Don't Put Lipstick on the Cat!

DON'T PUT LiPSTICK ON THE CAT!

WindRiver Publishing
St. George, Utah

Queries, comments or correspondence concerning this work should be directed to the author and submitted to WindRiver Publishing at:

authors@windriverpublishing.com

Information regarding this work or other works published by WindRiver Publishing Inc., and instructions for submitting manuscripts for review for publication, can be found at:

www.windriverpublishing.com

Don't Put Lipstick On The Cat!

Copyright © 2003 by Debbie Farmer

Illustrations by Jana Christy (www.janachristy.com)

How Embarrasing was originally printed in *Family Fun Magazine*, April 2000. *The Other Woman* was originally printed in *Family Fun Magazine*, September 2000.

Library of Congress Control Number: 2003108954
ISBN 1-886249-07-5

First Printing, 2003

Printed in China by Regent Publishing Services Ltd. on acid-free paper

To Heather, Ben and Dave, for giving me endless material to write about, my editors for making it legible and my friends and fans for sustaining me through it all

Surviving the Chaos of Parenting

Over the years people have asked me all sorts of questions.

They've asked me everything from the basic, "Are boys easier than girls?" to the more complex, "Exactly what color *is* your hair supposed to be anyway?"

But the one question they ask me the most is, "Why in the world do you bother to write a weekly column about your family when you could just go out and get a real job?"

Well, I'll tell you.

One day in the mid 1990's, I sat down and wrote an essay about my daughter's third birthday. Then, on a whim, I submitted it to the local mother's club newsletter. And since no one immediately showed up at my house to take away my typewriter or break all of my pencils, I took it, like most new writers would, as a sign of encouragement and wrote another—and another.

Then pretty soon a funny thing happened. Parents started coming up to me at the mall or in the park and saying things like, "Hey, we get kicked out of nice restaurants, too."

In fact, the more columns I wrote, the more it became clear that I wasn't just writing stories about *my* family, I was writing about other families as well. Suddenly I wasn't the only person in the world with a child who went through a Gold Lamé phase, an Only Eat Blue Food phase and an It's Been Five Minutes so I Must Go Change My Clothes Again phase.

I had company. Lots and lots of company.

And now, seven years and 350 plus columns later, I still do.

In fact, the other day a slightly frazzled woman with four children approached me in the grocery store and said, "Remember the column you wrote about how you forgot to bring your son's stuffed bear to the kindergarten picnic, and then returned a library movie to the video rental store and a rented video to the library? Well," she paused, "I can't tell you how relieved I was to find out that it's not just *me*."

Now, tell me, what job could be better than that?

Debbie Farmer

Contents

Holidays are the Most Wonderful Time of the Year (and other fantasies)

Summertime and the Livin' Ain't So Easy

School Days, School Days, Dear Old Golden Rule Days

There's No One Quite Like Dear Ol' Dad

Much More Than I Need to Know

Mark My Words (and the furniture and the walls...)

A Few for the Road

LIFE'S LITTLE MYSTERIES

A Good Sport

I enrolled my three-year-old son in a beginning athletic program for preschoolers to introduce him to various popular sports. I figured it would teach him good sportsmanship skills, team cooperation, and physical discipline—and also make him tired enough to take a two-hour nap.

On the first day of class, my husband and I brought our son onto the field to meet his teammates who were practicing hitting line drives down center field.

"Maybe he'll be another Babe Ruth or Willie Mays," my husband said, "and earn an athletic scholarship to an Ivy League college and go on to make millions while becoming a baseball legend!"

The coach introduced himself and handed my son a baseball mitt. He considered it for a moment, then put it on his head like a jaunty little cap.

"This week we're going to learn about t-ball," the coach said. "We'll take turns catching, throwing, and hitting. Understand?"

"Yes, sir!" my husband shouted.

My son sat down on the grass with the mitt over his eyes. While I tried to coax him to play, my husband decided to set a good example by participating in the activities. By the end of the game he had hit two homeruns, pitched a no hitter, and learned how to slide into home plate. He staggered to the car after the game and collapsed on the seat.

The next week, the coach introduced flag football. My son looked excited as the coach tucked a colored scarf into his belt.

"The object is to get the ball to the end zone," the coach explained, "but if your flag is taken, you must freeze."

"This is more like it," my husband said as our son ran through the field. "I had a hunch our son was meant to be a professional quarterback."

My son gathered as many flags as he could and stuffed them into his belt. Then he ran across the field towards the play equipment, looking like a big, bright windsock.

I tried to lure him back as my husband made three touchdowns and kicked a field goal. His teammates took their thumbs out of their mouths long enough to give him a high five after the game.

Next week the coach focused on field hockey. The children had to hit a ball between two cones with a stick.

My husband beamed as our son grabbed a stick and swung at the ball, the air, and the orange cones marking the goal.

"See, he's improving."

Just as I was about to agree, he threw down the stick, put a cone on his head, and galloped across the field like a possessed unicorn. I chased him while my husband played defense against a team of four-year-olds.

By the final lesson I knew my son had more of a chance of winning the grand prize in a magazine sweepstakes than a sports scholarship.

"This just isn't working out," I told the coach.

"What do you mean?" the coach said. "His self-esteem has improved, his fast ball is major league quality, and he's scored the winning points for his team in hockey."

"Yeah, it's done wonders for my husband, but I'm not sure what it's doing for my son."

The coach looked at me. "You'd be surprised."

Then he divided the children into teams for soccer. They practiced kicking the ball while my son tossed it into the air. What a waste of time and money, I thought. It would've been just as effective to send my son to play in the park wearing a pair of plastic cones, a colored flag, and a baseball mitt.

Then the coach gently guided him to the goal. "Stand here and catch any ball that comes your way," he said simply. My son nodded and I held my breath.

Suddenly the ball flew towards him and he reached out and caught it.

"Touch down!" he shouted as his teammates cheered and gave him a high five. When I saw his face I knew the coach was right. He looked happy and proud—and just as surprised as I was.

Fashionably Early

This may come as no big surprise to some of you, but lately I've had a severe case of fashion confusion. Through the years, I've always been the type of person sewing in shoulder pads when everyone else was taking them out, or hemming up my pant legs while everyone else was cutting them off. But at least I knew where I stood. However now, according to the leading fashion magazines, I'm not hopelessly out of style after all. I'm merely ahead of my time. As incredible as it seems, the shoulder pads and pegged pants that have been residing in my closet since the Reagan administration actually place me one decade ahead of the current fashion craze.

I don't know about you, but I'm a little confused by all this. I'm not sure whether to rush out and re-buy the same tie-dyed shirts and bell-bottoms I had three decades ago or to hang onto my twenty-year-old gunnysack dresses so I'll be ready when the fashion world works its way up to the eighties—again. Frankly, I get a headache just thinking about it.

But I'm not the only who's confused.

For example, the other day I went to the store and said to a sales clerk we'll call Tiffany, "I'd like a pair of beige dress pants with a 31 inch inseam."

"Sure," Tiffany nodded enthusiastically. "Capri, taper, or floods?"

Depending on the decade you were born in, the thought of buying any one of these can be a very, very bad mistake. I wasn't sure what to say so I said again, "Could I please have a pair of beige dress pants with a 31 inseam?"

Tiffany looked around the store and said she would try to find some while I stood next to the register clutching my purse. After a while she came back with another salesperson.

"What were you looking for, Ma'am?" she asked.

"A pair of beige pants with a 31 inch inseam," I said.

She giggled then put her arm around Tiffany. They walked into the back room together and closed the door.

When they came back they had the store manager with them.

"May I help you," she asked.

"Beige dress pants with a 31 inseam please," I said weakly. "But I'll settle for a pair of black shorts."

A flicker of recognition flashed through her eyes. "Great!" she said. "Walking, Bermuda or Board?"

I finally bought the first thing I recognized: a plain, white t-shirt.

However, it's not only pants that confuse me. It's shoulder pads, too. They wouldn't be so bad if they stayed where they belonged, but nooooo. You never know whether they're coming or going or where they'll show up next. In the eighties they started out small, but just as I got used to wearing them, they got bigger. Then they were removed altogether. Now they're put in all sorts of unexpected places, like bras. While this may not sound so bad to some people, it's just this sort of thing that could eventually lead to the downfall of western civilization as we know it.

Fortunately, I've found one fashion rule that has remained consistent throughout the years: the more money you spend, the thinner you get. It never ceases to amaze me that if I buy really, really expensive jeans, I'm always a size or two smaller than when I left the house. Coincidence? I think not. Of course this doesn't resolve my fashion confusion, but it's nice to know if I bought a pair of jeans the price of, say, Louisiana, I could finally be a size six.

By now some of you are probably wondering why I'm wasting so much time worrying about fashion when I should be concerned about loftier things, like everlasting world peace and all that. And you're probably right. But deep down I'm not really all that concerned about being in style—partly because I'm a secure, self-confident, mature person who has grown comfortable with herself—and partly because I know that sooner or later, even if I do nothing at all, I'm bound to end up wearing the appropriate clothes in the correct decade.

I just hope I'm ready when it happens.

Shopping Cartless

It was a personal triumph of sorts for me. I made it all the way through a big discount store, cartless. Ordinarily I set my standards for personal triumphs a bit higher than this, but it seems that whenever I innocently enter a store to buy, say, a bottle of glitter glue, I reappear several hours later the new owner of sixteen pair of panty hose, a hibachi, three packs of AA batteries, a gold lamé purse and salad tongs.

Oh, it's not like I do this on purpose. Afterwards, as I emerge in the parking lot squinting in the bright sunlight, I'm never quite sure what happened. So I cling to the hope that perhaps it isn't my fault. Maybe the smell of freshly popped popcorn had hypnotized me into buying a new exercise bike. Or maybe the Musak version of "Strawberry Fields" had compelled me to hurl a flowered hat into my cart. Or maybe, just maybe, the lack of oxygen in the windowless building had deprived my brain into thinking I needed a set of pink blow-up chairs and a fluorescent lamp.

Whatever the reason, I wasn't really worried until the day my husband found out.

"Honey," he said waving the check book, "why is there an entry for two hundred dollars in here? Did you make some kind of mistake?"

"Of course not," I say. "What do you take me for? I spent that on my trip for the dry erase markers."

"What about this one for fifty-seven dollars?" he asked.

"Scotch tape."

"A hundred and eight-two dollars and sixty cents?"

"One beach towel and a five-pound bag of puppy chow."

"But we don't have a dog!"

I could tell by the way he was yelling that he was a little upset. At first, I thought about telling him all about the popcorn and the Beatle's music and all that, but I had a feeling he wouldn't understand. So I called my friend Julie instead.

"Oh, it happens to me all the time," she said. "All you need to do is to focus on the item you need, go straight to it, then immediately take it to the register without stopping. And for gosh sakes," she hissed, "don't get a cart."

That was when the tide turned, so they say. The next time I went to the store I bypassed the carts, picked up a bottle of shampoo then headed towards the register. And I would've made it if, too, if it wasn't for a porcelain carafe that I saw out of the corner of my eye. I grabbed it with my free hand and kept walking.

Then I spotted an espresso maker that happened to be on sale. I held it in the crock of my elbow. Then I quickly stuffed a magazine under my left arm and wedged a pack of gum underneath my chin.

When I arrived at the register I piled my merchandise on to the counter and said loudly to the cashier, "Just hand me the bags when you're through. I don't need a cart. No-sir-ee."

She nodded knowingly.

And I would've congratulated myself right then and there on being a savvy shopper, not manipulated into spending money by cheap marketing ploys—except my total came to ninety-seven dollars and thirty-two cents.

I blame it on the popcorn.

Eternal Youth

I have found the secret of eternal youth: have your mom move in down the street. Oh, I must admit that when she first moved so close it was a shock to see her on a daily basis after all these years on my own. After all, no one else ever tells me that I look tired or that I need to go see the dentist. But let me tell you! It's done wonders for my outlook. I haven't felt so young since I was, say, thirteen.

Now don't get me wrong, I didn't regress all at once. In fact I'm not quite sure how it happened. One day I was happily in my mid-thirties, holding down a job while taking care of a house and two children, and the next, I was getting advice from my mother on how to effectively floss my teeth.

I should've recognized the signs when I'd say something like, "I've finally worked out a plan to redistribute our contributions to our tax-deferred annuity which increases our non-taxable return to well over market value. What do you think?"

And my mom would reply, "That's nice, dear. Are you sure you're eating enough? You look a little thin."

One time I remarked on how the uncertainty of a global economy could affect the overall performance of the stock market, and she just looked at me and asked if I was using the water filter she gave me for my last birthday since, "You never know what's in tap water these days and it will help clear up your skin."

Although suddenly becoming a middle-aged teenager isn't necessarily bad, sometimes I find myself reacting in ways I can't explain—like automatically rejecting my mom's advice even though I know she's right. In fact, last night after a speech on how adding more fiber to my diet would increase the overall health of my digestive track, I caught myself thinking, "I won't and you can't make me!" And on top of that I'm having sudden urges to get my belly button pierced and have a giant Ying-yang tattooed on my lower back. And I've started listening to really loud rock music in the car.

And it's not just me. My friend Linda, a successful woman with three children and a master's degree in education, refuses to wear socks with her tennis shoes every time her mother comes to visit.

Luckily I manage to metamorphose back into a qualified adult when I'm around my children.

"Don't sit so close to the television," I say to my eight-year-old daughter. "It's bad for your vision."

But she just rolls her eyes and asks me when I'm going to stop worrying so much.

I want to look at her and say, "Never! I'm your mother and that's my job." But I have a feeling she wouldn't understand.

However, despite my best efforts, my transformation doesn't last long. Just when I'm getting used to being over the legal drinking age, my mom will come over and say something like, "Have you been getting enough sleep?" or, "Make sure you wear your jacket because it looks like it's going to rain."

And I want to roll my eyes and say, "Oh, Mom. When will you quit worrying?"

But I already know the answer. And besides, sometimes it's nice to feel thirteen again.

Through the Eyes of a Child

I know that some people can size up a person pretty quickly by the way they dress and the company they keep. But, frankly, I think you never really know a person until you see what kind of vacation pictures they take. I mean, let's face it, when people go on vacation they bring back reams of film containing pictures of things that no one else in the whole world, and possibly the entire universe, would be interested in. For instance, when my friend Julie went to Europe last summer, instead of snapping photographs of the Louvre or the Eiffel Tower or Stonehenge, she brought back thirty-two rolls of cathedral ceilings. *Ceilings*! For the ten years I've known Julie I had never suspected that she was this passionate about stained glass.

And that's not all. My friend Linda, who has no children of her own, has three photo albums filled with pictures of her cats, all taken during her vacation in Venice. Now I've always been a big animal lover and all that, but this somehow just seems, well, wrong.

But one of the best things about these pictures, despite their obvious flaws, is that they can't help telling us a great deal about the people who took them.

So, that said, I shouldn't have been too surprised when I got the roll of film back from my five-year-old son's first camping trip. I naïvely opened the envelope expecting to see pictures of the nightly campfire, the sun setting over the forest, and possibly even a deer or two. But instead, I saw an off-center picture of tennis shoes! And not even *his* tennis shoes mind you, but rather a pair someone had left behind in the cabin. Mystery shoes. But that's not all. As I went through the stack, I also found my son had taken a picture of his sleeping bag, a penny he found in the gravel next to the car, a leaf, an orange sock, a bag of marshmallows, a close up of his father's ear, the tree outside his cabin from six different angles, a crushed snail, a burned hotdog, something blurry, the backseat of the car, a Power Ranger toothbrush, his thumb, a piece of gum, and himself.

There was barely a sign of nature in the whole stack. I couldn't help thinking that if he wanted pictures of assorted junk, it would've been cheaper if he'd spent the weekend in the backyard taking pictures of the sandbox.

At least that's what I thought until I showed them to my friend Julie, the mother of three teenagers, who said simply, "There's nothing wrong with these." But of course, this is just the type of answer you'd expect from someone who photographs ceilings. Then she told me about the time her daughter went to Yosemite Valley and returned with dozens of rolls of film, all filled with photographs of the hotel, restaurant and gift shop; and about the time her son took his camera to a pro baseball game and returned with twenty-four pictures of cloud formations. However, I had a feeling she was just trying to make me feel better.

But then again, to a five-year-old boy, finding a penny is more exciting than seeing a squirrel. And, for gosh sakes, why would he waste his good film on something like, say, a herd of endangered water buffalo, when he could take a picture of cool tennis shoes? Or his shiny, new, green sleeping bag? Face it, things like beautiful sunsets and campfires can't compare to a bag of extra large marshmallows.

So I did what any good mother would do: I marked the date on the back of the pictures and slid them into our family vacation photo album—right after the five pages of ice sculptures I took last year on our cruise to the Bahamas.

Birthdaze

"You pulled off a great birthday party," my husband said as he closed the door behind the last five-year-old child. "All the kids had fun."

"Yes. Fun," I said, as I sat down for the first time since breakfast. "Would you like ice cream with your cake?"

He looked around, confused. "I just finished some, thanks." He shrugged. "See? You were worried about a houseful of five-year-olds for nothing."

"Yes. Nothing." I leaned back in the chair. "How about a balloon poodle?"

"What?"

"All right, you can have the balloon sword, just don't hold it over the birthday candles after they're lit."

"Honey," he said. "It's okay. Everybody's gone. The party's over."

"Gone?" I said. "Where? They'd better not be upstairs trying to send the cat down the laundry chute again. Vanilla or chocolate?"

"You just lie down and rest a while," he said, leading me to the sofa.

"But it's game time! For goodness sake hang the piñata before the clown leaves and the kids want to sit on the good furniture. I'll get the video camera in case someone smiles."

"Just relax." He pulled down the mini blinds.

"What are you doing?" I cried, reaching for the chord. "I can't see into the backyard. Open the blinds so I can make sure no one dresses the dog in my good lingerie again. Who's the tall, thin kid standing in the corner?"

"It's the halogen lamp."

My husband eased me back onto the sofa.

"Mommy?" A tiny voice called from the doorway. "I'm thirsty."

"Oh, come in! I'm so glad you came." I turned to my husband. "Who's that?"

"That's our son," my husband said. "He lives here."

"The drinks are in the kitchen—it's down the hall to the left. Help yourself."

My husband placed a warm towel on my forehead. "Would you like some soothing music?"

"On the count of three—after I light the candles."

He gently patted my arm. "There, there."

"Where's the short kid who couldn't find the bathroom? I haven't seen him since noon." I grabbed my husband's hand. "Do you hear a flushing sound?"

He shook his head.

"It must be the kazoos ringing in my ears," I said. "I'm going to clear a spot to open the presents before the parents start arriving. Just make sure no one tapes the bows to the cat."

"But . . ."

"You don't want a repeat of last year, do you? It took me hours to cut the adhesive out of her fur, and the neighbors thought we got a French poodle."

"Mommy?"

"Yes, Sweet pea? The bathroom's upstairs to the right. Check for a lost little boy while you're there." I paused. "By the way, have you met the rest of the family?"

"What's wrong with Mom? She's been like this since the candles wouldn't light and the cat licked the cake."

"Post traumatic birthday syndrome," my husband whispered.

"Huh?"

"I read it's a reaction some mothers have after hosting a party at home for their children," he explained.

"Why is she feeding cake to the lamp?"

"I'm not sure, but don't worry," he said. "I bet with plenty of rest, she'll forget all about it and be good as new in time for Christmas."

New and Natural Barbie

I thought it was a joke when I first heard Mattel planned to give Barbie a makeover by widening her hips, reducing her bust, and flattening her facial features. I was pleased my daughter would finally have a plastic role model that resembled me, but I couldn't believe a child would want a Barbie that couldn't fit into jeans, was constantly on a diet, and hung out in the camper wearing a muumuu in front of the television because she never got asked out by Ken.

Mattel planned on creating six new dolls with the new "natural and today look." This was a real turning point in the fashion world, although I wasn't sure if she was invented to show little girls a diverse standard of beauty, or if the other Barbies needed someone to make fun of. I couldn't imagine a doll with *my* natural and today look: purple calves, buns of cellulite, and a stomach with its own fanny pack.

I bought the updated Barbie for my daughter because I thought it would be good for her to have a realistic role model and I harbored a desperate, maternal hope she would transfer her idolization to me.

"It's a new Barbie!" my daughter said as she pulled the doll out the box.

"Mommy," said my three-year-old son pointing to the doll.

"I call her the 'Working Mother of Two Barbie'," I said. "Look in the box; I think she comes with a plate of leftovers and a thigh master."

"Where's her bathing suit?" My daughter shook the empty box.

"She doesn't have one," I said, "but she has a nice, sturdy pair of sensible shoes."

My daughter frowned.

I quickly tried to find something positive to say about a Barbie that needed support hose and an elastic waistband. "Look! She has a wardrobe just like Mommy's!" She didn't look impressed so I added, "and she's really, really smart, just like you."

She considered her new Barbie for a moment then said, "I'll call her Francine."

While my daughter introduced her to the other Barbies, I congratulated myself on making a brilliant purchase.

Everything was going great until Ken asked Francine out on a date.

"Mommy!" my daughter said, "we need to get Francine nicer clothes."

"But I have a dress just like that."

"She only has one outfit that fits," she said. "Jeans won't go on, and her feet are too wide for high heels."

I seized the teachable moment.

"Francine doesn't need to go anywhere with Ken," I said. "She's going to go to college and get a high paying job, so she can support herself without being dependent on a good looking, muscular man with plastic hair."

My daughter stared.

"She doesn't need new clothes or stiletto heels to be beautiful," I continued. "Her inner qualities like kindness, confidence, and integrity are what matter." I felt important and proud as I bestowed my motherly wisdom on my daughter.

She considered Francine for a moment, then tossed her over her shoulder into her closet.

"Ken will take Gymnastic Barbie instead."

Francine was dumped for a doll with good thighs. I cursed myself for making such a stupid purchase.

That night, when I went into my daughter's room to kiss her good night, I found Francine tucked in beside her and Gymnastic Barbie lying haphazardly on the floor.

"See, good legs aren't everything," I whispered. She gave me a puzzled look, then I adjusted her blanket and turned out the light.

Kid Myths

There comes a time in every child's life, usually around the fourth grade, where they get the Wake Up Call of Reality.

And who can blame them? Over the years we've asked them to believe in rabbits coming into the house at midnight bearing baskets of colored eggs and chocolate; a jolly man in a beard who drives a sleigh pulled by eight tiny, flying reindeer and who drops presents down people's chimneys; and a fairy that flits about at night giving out good money for used teeth.

Clearly, it's only a matter of time before they stand back and say, "Whoa! Just a minute here. What kind of jogging suit did you say the Easter bunny was wearing again?"

These kinds of questions are the first sign that the gig is up, so they say. The truly amazing thing is that most of the time, parents are shocked when this finally happens. So they panic and create even more fantastic lies to try to prolong the inevitable.

One day my friend Susie found herself explaining to her nine-year-old that the reason the Tooth Fairy forgot to come and take her tooth was because she'd dropped her gold lamé purse during another call and had gone back to look for it, leaving the rest of the calls to her assistant, the Easter bunny, who couldn't reach second story bedrooms because everyone knows that rabbits can't fly.

Of course, this is exactly the sort of reaction that immediately confirms a child's deepest suspicions.

Oh sure, you could avoid the whole issue by being open and honest from the get go. But how do you look a two-year-old in the eye and say something like, "You see honey, there is no such thing as Santa. Or fairies. Or friendly rabbits that deliver colored eggs in baskets. The whole thing is all just a tiny little—ha, ha—lie."

Some people opt for the "don't ask—don't tell" policy. But this can be risky. Take, for instance, my friend Linda. She still gives presents from Santa to her teenagers. Every year her children pretended to go along with it. And around and around it'll go, with no clear end in sight, until one Christmas morning someone finally snaps and blurts out, "Okay, okay, enough with the Santa thing already."

At least childhood beliefs aren't that far-fetched. I mean, the mental leap from believing, say, that you might become a millionaire by buying one lottery ticket for a dollar to believing that a miniature fairy flies around collecting old teeth isn't all that big, really. You can see how kids fall for this kind of stuff.

And it's not like we live in France. Why, I was reading just the other day about how French children believe that every Easter a special bell flies up from Rome just to deliver chocolate candy. A FLYING BELL! And this coming from the same culture that gave us Dom Pérignon and Renoir?

But I digress.

The funny thing is, the Wake Up Call of Reality doesn't happen all at once. Ask any parent, there's no rhyme or reason to it. A ten-year-old who dismisses the existence of Santa and flying reindeer as merely a laughable idea might still believe in, say, the Tooth Fairy.

So I wasn't too surprised the day my eight-year-old son sidled up to me as if he were going to whip out a collection of used watches from underneath his trench coat.

"Psst," he whispered. "I know there's no such thing as Santa." He stood back and waited for my reaction.

"Oh, really?" I said. "Okay."

"Or the Tooth Fairy," he threw in for good measure.

That left Leprechauns, the Easter Bunny, and possibly the Great Pumpkin. Three out of five. Hey, I can live with that.

Selling the Family Car

Now, if you've never tried selling a car, let me just say that it's not as simple as you'd think. I mean you can't just drive the car down to the corner lot and toss up a sign and go on about your business. It can be a very delicate and time-consuming process.

This is mainly because you have to first get the car "acceptable for public viewing."

So on a sunny Saturday morning, I enticed the kids to help by corralling them onto the driveway along with the hose and buckets. Of course this brought up a whole new set of problems, the main one being that unwrapping the hose is the universal cue for kids to magically disappear, only to reappear minutes later dressed in swim suits and hauling inflatable water toys.

Sure, I could've said something ridiculous like, "Hey, how about helping me wash the car?" But I would be naïve to think that something this simple would work with my family. So, to the surprise of absolutely no one, I washed it myself.

And I would've been okay with it, really, but just when things were coming along nicely, I did something that you should never ever do alone—or without being under the influence of prescription medication—I removed the car seat.

You always hear warnings about this kind of thing but you never really believe them. I found (and I'm not kidding here) someone's wet sock, a key, a handful of French fries having a bad hair day, an art project made out of jelly beans, several pieces of gum dating back to the Reagan years, and four mystery wads of Kleenex containing something yucky that had to be spit out by a kid.

Let me just say that it's things like this that make you wonder just where, exactly, you went wrong. I mean, back when the car was new, there used to be strict sets of rules to follow, like: no eating or drinking, no kicking the seat in front of you, no putting shoes on the dashboard, no yelling, no spitting, no strapping the cat into the front seat, and no entering until you've been patted down for anything that looks like, once was, or somehow could be, turned into a crumb.

However, we all know these things never last. But the freaky thing is that the change happens so slowly you hardly even notice.

First there's a harmless cheese stick. Then come a few contraband grapes. After that you move up to fruit roll-ups and, what the heck, raisins. From there it isn't such a big leap to Baggies full of Cheerios and goldfish crackers. Before you know it, entire Cub Scout troops are sitting in the back seat singing bawdy playground songs and swigging juice boxes. So, really, you can see how these things happen.

And the really freaky thing is you hardly notice how far you've gone until one day—The Day of Reckoning, I call it—you have to make the car "acceptable for public viewing." And by then (you guessed it) it's too late.

However, it's not all bad news. The good news about The Day of Reckoning is that you usually find some real treasures. As luck would have it, I found a gold earring, a pack of lifesavers, and over three dollars in pennies. And, oh yeah, an attachment from the old car vacuum.

And the rest of the stuff? Well, I'd like to say I got rid of it once and for all, but instead I did what any desperate and slightly weary parent would do: I shoved it deeper into the cushions and strapped the car seat back in.

Then I got into my bathing suit and borrowed my daughter's swim fins.

The Vortex of Lost Stuff

At least once per day, without fail, something in my house disappears. I'm not sure why this happens but I've begun to suspect that somewhere in my house is a sort of alternate reality, a special warp in the universe, where car keys and socks and cell phones slip through when no one is looking.

Sure, it sounds crazy, but then tell me, what else can explain why so many objects vanish into thin air?

In fact, it happens so often that I've begun to walk aimlessly around the house with what my family has come to know as my "looking for lost stuff" expression, a combination of slack jaw, glazed eyes, and vacant stare.

As shocking as it may seem, this not a particularly useful sort of system, but I have learned some helpful tips on what *not* to do when your things are suddenly sucked to into the Vortex of Lost Stuff.

Do not check the garbage can, the diaper pail, behind the sofa cushions or inside the dishwasher for your car keys. THEY ARE NOT THERE.

Don't bother wasting your time trying to think where you last saw them, thinking somehow they will magically reappear. Everyone knows that the number one rule of Lost Stuff is that nothing, NOTHING ever reappears in the same exact spot it disappeared in.

Do not try to retrace every waking moment of your day, including every time you changed the baby or your big trip down the driveway to the mailbox. This kind of close scrutiny into what your life is really like will only confuse and depress you.

Do not, under any circumstance, enlist outside help. It's not only useless, it makes you feel, well, stupid. I mean, when was the last time you called a department store about losing your cell phone and the person who answered said, "Why, yes! In fact, I found one fitting exactly that description, and I put it in my pocket with all of the other cell phones I've found on the floor today."

My conversations go more like this:

"Hello. I was in earlier today and I lost . . ."

"Oh, hi, Mrs. Farmer," the clerk says. "No I haven't found a phone, a jacket, a pair of glasses or any keys."

But let me just say, there's nothing worse than losing your child's orthodontic headgear. Not only do you have to put more money into a mouth that has already cost about the same as say, Monaco, the orthodontist calls you in to the office and makes you sit on a little stool next to the patient's chair as if *you* (ha! ha!) are somehow responsible.

"So how is everything going with the headgear?" he asks in a sly, knowing sort of way.

This is a sure sign that your credibility is shot. You've now become marked as a Person Who Can't Keep Track of Things. No matter what you say, he'll think you run a shoddy kind of household with lost headgears lying about in the potted plants and stacks of overdue library books propping up the weak corners of your end tables.

It's then that I'm tempted to tell him all about the warp in reality and the Vortex of Lost Stuff and how nothing in this world is safe from being sucked into an invisible, alternate plane of the universe the minute no one is looking.

But, instead, I mumble "Oh, fine. Thanks." And head quietly to the counter with my checkbook to buy a new one.

And it's not because I'm too embarrassed to admit to this crazy, superstitious way of thinking, mind you, but rather because I've got to hurry home and keep an eye on the new DVD player.

I just hope it's not too late.

YOU CAN'T FiGHT MOTHER NATURE

⊛f Mice and (Wo)men

I know you might think it's silly for a woman who went through natural childbirth twice to be scared of a harmless little mouse—but I, like most people in the current century, prefer my rodents outside.

It was only yesterday that I was downstairs in the living room innocently minding my own business folding laundry, when I saw a shadow gallop across the floor out of the corner of my eye.

I did what any educated, independent woman would do: I yelled, "Yeeeeekkkkk!" Then I ran upstairs and locked myself into my office.

When my husband came home from work, I casually explained to him how I wouldn't normally be afraid of something so harmless, and the reason I'm sitting on top of my desk is because this particular mouse is part of an unusually large species that looks more like small Chihuahuas.

"Well, where is it?" he asked.

"I have no idea. For all I know he could be in the dishwasher, underneath the refrigerator, or in my closet trying on shoes," I said dryly. "Just get him!"

An hour later he walked back into my office.

"You can come out now," he announced triumphantly. "He's gone."

"Great! Did you dispose of the b-o-d-y?" I whispered. When he didn't answer, I became suspicious. "You didn't find it, did you?"

He slowly shook his head. "But since I didn't see it, it's obviously gone."

Now you might think I'm being overly cynical here, but I wasn't convinced. This theory might've worked if he'd been looking for something a little bigger like, say, an elephant, but it was clear to me that this mouse was obviously lying low, waiting for another chance to strike. Why, at this very moment, it was probably lurking under the kitchen table waiting for me to open the refrigerator door so it could charge over my feet and eat up all my expensive cheese—or sleeping underneath my comforter—or, for gosh sakes, living in my closet making a nest inside my good pumps.

So I weighed my alternatives and figured I could (a) move, (b) hire a professional exterminator, or (c) remain locked in my office until the mouse eventually got bored and wandered away of its own accord.

I finally decided on a less complicated plan that consisted of searching every corner of the house with a flashlight, then trying to scare it to death by waving my hands around and screaming. So I pulled myself together and looked in every closet and underneath every piece of furniture, trying to determine if the mouse was there, had been there, or could possibly show up there at any moment.

Then, when I was about to give up and think that maybe, just maybe, my husband had been right, I saw a mouse-shaped shadow dart across the floor out of the corner of my eye.

I immediately sprang into action, but the only ones affected by my plan were my children.

"Mommy are you okay?" they asked.

Just when I was ready to put my house up for sale and live in a hotel until the real-estate market picked up, my friend Julie suggested getting one of those "humane" mouse traps that's really more like a plastic box with clear sides and a door.

According to the directions, all I would need to do is lure the mouse into the container, then drive it to a nice empty field and release it back into nature. I pictured myself bravely watching as the mouse ran off into the distance, just like the woman in the heart-wrenching scene from *Born Free* after she releases the lion she raised into the jungle to fend for itself.

So I bought the humane trap, confident it was the only good and decent thing to do.

The next morning I was still confident about my decision—until I was faced with the actual possibility of having to drive around the neighborhood looking for a field, with a mad mouse trapped inside a flimsy plastic box, seat-belted into the front seat of my car.

Now, I'm not a religious person, but as I walked down the stairs to check the box I silently prayed, "Dear God, I promise I'll do better. I'll be more kind and patient toward others. I'll donate more money to charity and even make both of my children's birthday cakes from scratch; but please, please don't let there be a live mouse in that box. Amen."

As I bent down and peered into the box, I imagined seeing a vindictive ten-pound mouse with beady eyes and sharp teeth, glaring at me if it were trying to decide whether it should wait until I let it loose to tear me to shreds, or to just go ahead and open the box itself and get it over with quickly.

So, when I saw that it was empty I felt like throwing my hands out to my sides and bursting into song. However, it also meant that the mouse was still loose somewhere in my house.

But between you and me, now I think I can learn to live with it.

A Cat's Best Friend

My friend Shirley is a sucker for stray animals. I don't know why, but at any given time you can find at least five strange dogs lounging in her backyard. In fact, most of the dogs look so content I have a hunch that they really aren't lost at all, they're merely on vacation. They just wait for their owners to turn their backs, then dash straight to Shirley's house for a bit of relaxation, good food, and a nice change of scenery. Call me weird, but I could never fully understand why such a strong, sane person like Shirley could let animals walk all over her like that.

Of course, that was before my family was taken hostage by a stray cat. Now normally an occasional cat in the backyard wouldn't be a problem, but I could tell by the way it peered into the window and meowed for five hours straight that it wasn't just passing through. For some reason I couldn't understand, this cat wanted desperately to come inside our house.

Now I've always loved cats, but any animal that voluntarily chooses to live with my family has to be a little, well, off. Oh, it's not like we're bad people. But there is nothing, nothing about us that says we need a new cat. Or want a new cat. In fact, I don't even have a good track record with pets. My childhood was a blur of hamsters followed by a plethora of goldfish and hermit crabs that all met untimely, tragic deaths. I still carry the guilt around to this day.

But try explaining that to a stubborn fifteen-pound cat clinging onto your back screen door.

"I wonder why it wants to come in so badly?" my daughter asked.

"Maybe it's lost," my husband said.

"Or maybe it just wants someone to pet it," my son said.

My theory is that perhaps the mounds of broken plastic toys, baskets of dirty laundry, and crumbs mashed into the carpet had confused the cat into thinking my living room was really a deserted back alley somewhere on the shady side of town.

At first I tried ignoring it. When that didn't work, I did the only thing I could think of—I fed it. Now, I know that's exactly the kind of thing people are always warning you about, but I figured since it was already meowing at the same volume as say, a Metallica concert, there was no harm in giving it a little snack.

"Don't worry, it'll be okay," I assured my husband. "You'll see."

By the next morning the cat had torn the screen off the sliding door and begun circling the house in an obsessive, Kathy Bates sort of way.

At one desperate point, I called my neighbor Julie, who has five cats. "Say, you aren't missing a particularly persistent cat with a fluffy orange tail, are you?"

"No, why?"

"There's one outside trying to break in."

"So, let it in."

Now even I know that once you let a cat in, any type of freedom you had is over. It is now *your* cat. In fact, I bet the word would be out on the street in minutes and tomorrow I would find five more cats circling my house. Then ten. And pretty soon I'd become one of those ladies who has cats milling around on top of the refrigerator, hiding behind the washing machine, and sleeping in the potted plants.

So I put a scary look on my face, looked the cat straight in the eye, and said firmly, "Go away."

And that would've been the end of it, except for the fact that the cat purred, then walked between my legs and into the house.

So I decided to let it stay. But just for a little while. After all, I'm a mature adult and I can handle one small cat without letting it take over my life.

Oh, and about what I said earlier about Shirley—if you don't mind, let's just keep that between you and me.

_A_ Fly on the Wall

You'll be shocked to learn that as of yesterday afternoon, we have a new addition to our family: a six-legged, bubble-eyed, two-winged housefly named Kellie.

Although I'm not sure why my son has started adopting household insects, I have a hunch it's either the result of a recent onslaught of children's animated bug movies, or the delayed side effects from the painkillers administered during his birth.

Like most people, I prefer my bugs outside. But I agreed to go along with it since I thought this was a cute display of his imagination. After all, how long could he be interested in something that can't fetch or make facial expressions? At least that was what I thought yesterday—before Kellie had her own place at the dinner table and my son insisted on feeding her all of the expensive cheese.

After the initial attraction cooled off, most of my son's relationship with Kellie revolved around keeping her from flying away.

We couldn't open a door or window without my son charging after us to close it.

But with all the trouble we had keeping Kellie from going out, I couldn't understand how three more flies had managed to sneak in.

"Look!" my son cried. "It's Kellie's family!"

I stopped letting anyone who wasn't a close family member into the house; I had a feeling that when I explained to them that my house was full of flies (because I can't figure out which one is my son's new pet, Kellie) they'd sign me up for a twelve step program at the nearest rehab center. All I could do was, (a) hope the flies would eventually go away, (b) try to figure out which one was Kellie, or (c) swat them all and hope I could afford the bills for my son's years in therapy.

I finally decided to call the only people I knew would understand: my friends with children. As I suspected, my best friend Shirley told me about the time her daughter put a lady-bug collection in the crisper to eat the good lettuce because, "They looked hungry." And my friend Judy assured me that her son had once brought home a lizard named Steve and stored him under the tissue paper in one of her shoeboxes—with her good pumps still in it.

I knew they were just trying to cheer me up. But despite their help, I had a hunch (and I may be wrong about this) that we're the only family in the world to be on a first name basis with a fly.

"Maybe we can teach it a trick and get it a guest spot on David Letterman," my husband suggested.

"Very funny," I said. But I wasn't really worried. According to the *Animal Planet* show, flies have a life span of around two days. And sure enough, the next morning all four of them were lying on the windowsill with their little feet up in the air.

Although I was relieved, I was concerned about how my son was going to take the death of his first pet. What if he took it hard? What if handling it incorrectly led to deep psychological problems in the future? What if, for gosh sakes, he wanted a funeral?

"Kellie was a good pet," I said gently. "And I know you'll miss her."

"Yeah," my son nodded. "But that's okay, Mom." He reached into his pocket and pulled out a small garden snail. "I still have Lisa."

Good-bye, Kellie. Rest in peace.

Getting a Little Crabby

Last weekend I took my children to a local outdoor fair that had live music, craft booths and games. We started in the children's section where the first booth we saw was decorated with a colorful display of bright starfish and seahorses.

"Look, mom!" my daughter cried. "If I throw a ball into the bowl I can get a hermit crab!" She looked at me with big, pleading eyes as I reached into my pocket and handed the attendant a quarter for five balls.

A pet might not be a bad thing, I thought as she leaned over and tossed her first ball. It might teach her about caring, empathy, and responsibility. Besides, what were her chances of making it in?

Her first four shots missed and I already started backing away when she turned and handed the last ball to me.

"Mommy, will you try? Please?"

I nodded. Then I closed my eyes, wound my pitch, and threw it as hard as I could—away from the bowls.

"You made it!" my daughter cried, throwing her arms around my neck. "You won a hermit crab!"

My daughter looked into the tank and picked a perky crab that was crawling around on top of the others. Then the attendant put it in the Styrofoam container and handed me a piece of paper.

"These are the instructions for a healthy and happy crab," she said. "Read them carefully."

I folded the directions and stuffed them into my purse. After all, I raised two children. How hard could it be to take care of one tiny crab?

When we got home from the fair, I opened the container.

"Why isn't it moving?" my daughter asked.

"Maybe it's asleep." I quickly found the directions and began to read: "Hermit crabs should be kept moist in a terrarium with vented covers." I got back into the car and drove to the local pet store before my daughter's twenty-five cent crab turned into a year of therapy bills.

I ran through the door and approached the woman at the counter. "I need help," I cried. "Fast!"

The woman nodded knowingly. "The hermit crab terrariums are in the back."

When I left the store I had so many supplies I could barely carry them to the car. In addition to the terrarium I had a spray bottle to keep the hermit crab moist, a five pound bag of gravel so it could dig, a plastic deep-sea diver to keep it from getting lonely, and three extra shells in different sizes in case it molted and had an identity crisis. I could've bought ten crab leg dinners for the same price.

When I got home I prepared the terrarium, then called my daughter to see the crab thrive in its new environment.

"Why isn't it moving?" my daughter asked, peering through the glass.

"Maybe it's hungry." I grabbed the paper off the table and read: "Hermit crabs need a balanced diet of protein and calcium. They especially like organic peanut butter, fresh fruit and cheese."

As I staggered into the kitchen to prepare its meal, I wondered why I always refused to get a nice low-maintenance dog that ate table scraps and licked the crumbs off the dining room floor.

Twenty minutes later I emerged with peanut butter and banana pâté spread on a hunk of Brie cheese. I tossed it into the terrarium. We watched as the crab took a step towards it, took a bite, and crawled back into its shell.

"Cool!" my daughter cried.

I picked up the instruction sheet and tried to find the part about hermit crab indigestion—then I saw the fine print along the bottom. I read, "By following these simple care instructions, you will keep your hermit crab for many wonderful years of enjoyment." I tried to interpret what they considered to be "many," and I figured this was going to be the most expensive, high maintenance pet we ever had.

"Look! It moved again!"

"That's nice, honey," I said weakly. Then I crumpled up the paper, staggered to the sofa, and vowed next time there was an outdoor fair in the neighborhood, my family wasn't leaving the house.

All in the Name of Science

Hard as this may be to believe, I've intentionally become the owner of ants. Fifty of them, give or take a few. Now some of you may be wondering what I'm doing with all these insects, but those of you with children will instantly suspect that a birthday gift from a well-meaning childless relative is behind all this. And you'd be right.

I mean, if anyone had tried telling me that one day I'd pay good money to watch a bunch of ants (the very same type I see everyday in my kitchen for free) build tunnels in a plastic terrarium, I'd think they'd been varnishing wood furniture without the windows open again.

But stranger things have been done in the name of science. Or so they say. And certainly giving my children a hands-on educational experience is a worthy goal.

That said, the first lesson we learned about keeping an Ant Farm is that you just can't round up a few strays from underneath the kitchen sink and herd them all into a container and call it science. Oh no. You need special ants that you must mail order from a P.O. Box in New Jersey.

So while we all waited for these ants to arrive, we busied ourselves preparing the terrarium. Needless to say, we tried to make it as natural and ant-like as possible. We added the sand and several decorative accessories that came in the box like, for example, several miniature plastic shops, a couple of trees, two tiny plastic sports cars, and something that looked like a miniature gazebo with an adjustable swing.

"What are the ants going to do in *there*?" my husband asked. "Date?"

"Don't get smart," I said.

When the ants finally arrived my children eagerly placed them in their new home. Okay, perhaps "placed" is too mild a word. Rather we forced them in through the tiny hole in the top of the terrarium by flinging them off the top of a pencil.

"They don't look so good," my son said.

"I bet they're hungry," my daughter offered.

Of course this brought up a whole new set of problems. You see, according to the official care instructions, instead of eating the usual things like potato chips and stale breadcrumbs, these ants preferred the Bhatkar diet. For those of you lucky enough not to know what this is, it's a special ant food formula named after, you guessed it, Awinash Bhatkar who, I suspect, had way too much time on his hands.

Anyway, according to the recipe, all we had to do was create a mixture of "1 egg, 62 ml honey, 1 gm vitamins, 1 gm minerals, 5 gm agar salts, and 500 ml water." Once we figured out what, exactly, agar salt was, we had to dissolve it in 250 ml of boiling water. Next we mixed the water, honey, vitamins, minerals, and the egg together until smooth. After that we added the agar (stirring constantly), then poured the mixture into Petri dishes (0.5-1cm deep) and stored them in the refrigerator.

Let me just say, I have soufflé recipes that are easier to prepare.

However, despite all the hard work, I must admit we did learn a thing or two about ants. For instance, we learned that, 1) the expensive ones you mail order from New Jersey look suspiciously similar to the free California ones in my kitchen, 2) most of them would rather live just about anywhere than inside a terrarium, no matter how good the shopping is, and 3) ants are way too short to push each other on a swing.

Oh yeah, I learned one more thing.

If you leave the lid off the container, the ants will eventually escape and thrive on their own by eating the cookie crumbs underneath the refrigerator.

It's funny how science works.

_A_ Black Thumb

Like most people, I haven't lived all these years on this planet without becoming confused about a thing or two.

But, I admit, one of the things that confuses me the most is why people keep trusting me to take care of their houseplants. Oh, it's not like I don't like flora and fauna and all that, but let's just say I'm the sort of person who has trouble maintaining the delicate balance of nature.

Oh sure, there are occasional success stories about exceptionally hearty plants that have withstood my care, but for the most part, the ones with the highest survival rate at my house are of the _Silkea plastica_ variety.

But just try explaining this to desperate people who need you to take care of their houseplants so they can go away on vacation. Go ahead, try it.

If you're anything like me, you won't have the heart to say no and you'll somehow end up getting talked into doing it as a (_ha, ha_) favor.

Sure, the directions seem simple enough. "All you have to do is water it twice a week," they'll call as they drop it on my doorstep with the car running, "And it should be fine."

Fat chance.

Of course, the plant will start out looking good. Maybe even great. It might even look pretty sitting in your living room on your bookshelf. However, don't let this act fool you.

For example, take a particularly sensitive potted bougainvillea I'll call Justine. A year ago I got stuck watching her while my friend Barb went to the Bahamas. Now that just shows my bad attitude. I shouldn't say, "Got stuck." I think I may have accidentally volunteered. I'm sure I was thinking that it wouldn't be so bad. And it wasn't.

But sometime around the third day living with my family, her leaves shriveled and went brown. This should've been my first clue that something was wrong.

So I moved her into the kitchen where there was more light. The next day she lost her flowers. I gave her some vitamins. Then she went limp. I sprayed her with organic fungicide to kill earwigs and mites. She grew scaly. I put her underneath a heat lamp on my nightstand and read her chapters from a steamy romance novel. She died.

Frankly, I could never quite forgive myself.

When Barb came back, I broke the bad news and offered to buy her a new one.

"Oh, that's okay," she said a little too brightly. "Really."

Then she backed away and ran for her car.

Soon after that, the word was out on the street that I was a willing plant sitter. The next thing I knew my friend Linda dropped off her high-maintenance topiary. This was followed by my neighbor Pat's temperamental tomato plant, and then a mysterious, slightly hostile bonsai tree.

All of which I killed off almost immediately.

Which makes me wonder why people still bring me their plants to watch. Call me crazy, but I'm beginning to suspect that maybe, just maybe, people don't want them back. That my house has become, in fact, some kind of dumping ground for unmanageable houseplants.

As crazy as this sounds, it would sure explain a lot of things like, say, why my friend Tammy has never picked up the out-of-control fichus tree she dropped off before she left on vacation last spring, and why I found three nervous-looking fuchsias sitting on my doorstep this morning.

Of course, this could all be just my imagination. Maybe odd forces are at work and people actually trust me because they think I'm good with plants.

And, really, I am getting better with them. In fact, the other day, I think I actually bonded with a philodendron. Well, at least, I watered it and it didn't die.

All right, so it might've been a coincidence. But sometimes, with nature, that's enough.

(Go Take a Hike

Summer is a puzzling season. On one hand, you can get away with staying up late, forgetting your turn in the carpool, and serving blue popsicles for dinner. On the other hand, you have to work twice as hard to find stimulating activities to keep your children busy. And believe me, no matter how hard I try, there are few things in this world that my five-year-old son, Ben, and my eight-year-old daughter, Heather, will do together.

Take last year for example. By the second week of vacation we had already checked out twelve library books and visited the zoo three times. By the third week the wading pool had sprung a leak and was listing to one side and by week four, my children were arguing over things like who had the most peanut butter on their sandwich and whose turn it was to pet the cat. They'd watched so many episodes of *Animal Planet* they could tell the difference between a Banded Greenhouse Thrip and a Stump Slug. I knew I had to think of something fast before they got really bored and turned on me.

That's when I remembered a regional park about ten miles away with several hiking trails. What could be better than packing lunches and spending the day chasing butterflies, splashing through streams and smelling wildflowers?

"Ah, mom, do we really have to go?" Heather said, rolling her eyes.

"I don't want to," Ben crossed both arms over his chest.

"Come on, it'll be fun," I said. "And you can each bring a new disposable camera to take pictures with."

Their eyes lit up and I knew I'd won.

The next morning we dispersed to fill our backpacks with essential survival supplies: I took food, water, and Band-Aids. Ben packed his metal fire engine and Heather took a bottle of nail polish and a tube of Cotton Candy Pink lipstick. Great. If we encountered a wild animal on the trail, I could hypnotize it with the flashing red light, then hold it down and give it a beauty treatment while one of the kids ran for help.

When we arrived at the park, Heather and Ben were so excited about seeing nature that they immediately pulled out their disposable cameras and began taking pictures of other people's cars.

"Isn't this wonderful?" I said. The weather was balmy, the breeze refreshing and the air smelled like grass and flowers. I put my arms straight out to my sides and twirled around like a windmill.

"I'm hungry," Ben said.

"Just look at that giant tree," I cried, dragging him onto one of the more populated trails. "I think I see a Banded Greenhouse Thrip."

"I'm hungry, too," Heather said.

I finally gave in and at 9:30, we sat down at the head of the trail and ate lunch. I began to think that my children were determined to spend the rest of the summer watching television and arguing over peanut butter. Then I had an idea: I picked up a leaf, put a napkin over it, and gently rubbed it with cotton candy pink lipstick.

"Hey, a pink leaf," Ben said. "Cool!"

After lunch we started down the trail and made rubbings of leaves, tree bark and anything else we found in our way. We eventually ran out of napkins and lipstick, but we kept walking anyway.

"Hey, look at that tree!" Ben leaned back and took a picture of it while Heather looked up at the sky and put her arms straight out to her sides and spun around like a windmill. They were so immersed in what they were doing they didn't realize how far we had hiked. In fact, I didn't either, until we got back to the car and I felt the muscles in my thighs begin to cramp and red hot pain shooting through the bunions in my feet.

"Mom, why are you limping like that?" my daughter asked. "Are you okay?"

"Of course," I said, easing my blistered feet into the car.

When we got home I had the film in the disposable cameras developed. We mostly had pictures of strangers, the undersides of tall trees, and cars.

But my favorite picture was the one I took with my camera: Heather and Ben kneeling over a napkin in the dirt, happily making pink leaf rubbings—together.

Spider Season

This is an exceptionally busy time of year for me because, you see, it's officially spider season. I know this because this morning I found one lurking on the wall behind the toaster—waiting, I suspect, for me to finish my cup of coffee before making its move to take over the kitchen.

All right. I know what you're thinking. You're thinking that no self-respecting person would be afraid of a little spider. Snakes, mice, big dogs—sure. But a spider? You're thinking that everyone knows that most of the time they're harmless and eat annoying insects and at least in classic children's literature have a heart of gold. On top of that you're thinking that I could be better utilizing my time by worrying about real dangers like, say, the skyrocketing crime rate, global warming, and the increasing national debt because, you see, no one has ever been mugged by a wolf spider in his or her kitchen. And yes, on some deeper level I know this. But, hey, it's a spider. A SPIDER!

Everyone knows what seeing one wandering around loose in the house means. It means that, most likely there are millions, perhaps trillions, of other ones still in hiding. They're hanging out in your good shoes or in the back of the hall closet, biding their time quietly spinning webs until one day you awake to find all of your daughter's Barbies wrapped inside an exceptionally large cocoon and the cat tied to the television antenna.

So it follows that during spider season, I have to be especially vigilant. I have to inspect every corner of my house for spider webs and then determine, 1) how long ago it was made, 2) how big the spider was that made it, and 3) if the original owner is gone for good or merely on vacation and if so, where exactly did it *go*?

But really, even if I knew I still wouldn't be safe because, you see, I made the mistake of living on a planet that everyone knows is full of spiders.

Face it, with spiders you mostly have two choices. The first is that you can always find a big stick and, as they say in some circles, "whack it." However, this is not only vicious and cruel, everyone knows if you miss you will then have a really mad spider limping around your house, rousing all of the others into some kind of horrible retaliation. Besides, what kind of example is that for your children?

The second, much more politically correct choice is to simply relocate it. Preferably by air to the next state. But of course, this would involve coming close enough to touch it. My friend Shirley is good at this. One time she used nothing but a yellow sticky note to scoop up a particularly persistent gray spider and deposit it on the front lawn—where it took two days to make its way back into the house and the whole thing started again.

The good news is, if neither of these choices is for you, you can always yell "AHHHHHHHHHHH," then run into the bathroom and lock the door.

I'm not sure how good this idea works yet. But I must say that so far, there's no sign of any spiders in here. And, yes, I'll come out eventually.

Just as soon as spider season is over!

AN ADVOCATE FOR THE DOMESTICALLY CHALLENGED

House Rebellion

I have to type this story fast because, you see, I haven't got much time. Now, normally I can take as long as I like, leisurely typing a few words here and there in-between wandering around the house and gazing into the refrigerator. I can mull over my every word before I set it down on paper. But not today. Nuh-uh. You see, last week my husband finished filing our tax return and in the heat of the moment, turned to me and said loudly, "Honey, I think we might be getting a refund this year."

"Shhhh!" I hissed. "Don't you remember what happened the last time you said something like that?" I quickly clamped my hand over his mouth before the house could hear. I hoped maybe, just maybe, it had been preoccupied with things like settling and forming new cracks.

But, sure enough, the next day when I came home, the garage door opener wouldn't work. No matter how hard I pushed the button the door remained shut as if saying to me, "Just try to get into your house, lady. I dare you." So I did what any other intelligent, educated person would do in my situation: I repeatedly hit the remote control against the side of the steering wheel.

Eventually my husband came home and we pried the door open, but I've been around long enough to know what this means. It won't be long before the other appliances catch on about the extra money being spent on the garage door and I'll be spending my days shopping for new bolts and wires and calling repairmen.

And if you don't believe me, just ask my neighbor, Julie. Once her husband had briefly mentioned a Christmas bonus over dinner and sure enough, the next day her dishwasher wouldn't start. And just as soon as they had that fixed, the upstairs plumbing started leaking and the furnace gave out.

My friend Tina made the mistake of announcing that she was going to put part of her new pay raise away for a cruise. Then the next thing she knew, her washing machine was overflowing and seeping into the living room underneath her new carpet.

On the other hand, my friend Jenny is careful to never mention extra money out loud and she's lived in the same house for ten years without so much as replacing the furnace filter.

So even though I was careful not to mention anything about the new garage door opener within earshot of the rest of the house, I wasn't too surprised when the heat mechanism in my dryer went out the next day. Or when the vacuum cleaner belt broke.

But when I went to pick up my daughter from school and the car wouldn't start, that was the last straw.

When my husband came home, I grabbed him by the collar. "Tell the house that you were only kidding about the tax r-e-f-u-n-d," I begged.

"What?" He eyed me suspiciously. "Have you been varnishing the wood furniture again?"

"Just do it! Quick!" I let out a crazy little laugh.

So far, it's been two hours since anything has broken, refused to move or made funny noises. Oh, I realize our appliances don't really know when we have extra money, and it's only just a coincidence that they're breaking down all at once. But I'm not taking any chances. I'm typing this story as fast as I can—just in case my computer catches on.

In the Bag

Every day I try to send my daughter to school with a home-made lunch just like my mother used to make. I put it in a colorful bag along with a special message that she can read while she eats.

Unfortunately, my high expectations slowly descend into the abyss of reality during the course of the week, and my daughter can tell what day it is by the content of her lunch bag.

On Monday I am perky and bright-eyed. I snap open her lunch bag and ponder the four food groups. I lovingly prepare a bunch of juicy grapes, two different kinds of homemade cookies, a container of soup, a bottle of fresh squeezed orange juice and a sandwich (which I trim into fun little shapes with cookie cutters).

I contemplate her note: "Darling princess, you are the light of my life. Do your best work at school. I will see you when you get home. Lots of love, Mom." I can barely find enough room in the bag to slide it in.

On Tuesday, I'm a little less perky. I set her bag on the counter and try to recycle what is leftover from Monday. I add more water to the soup and stuff the remaining pieces of homemade cookies into a baggie. We're running late so I substitute the grapes with a box of raisins. I barely have time to cut her sandwich in half before closing the bag. I quickly add a note: "Do your best as you always do. I am proud of you. Love, Mom."

By Wednesday some of the food is already gone, so I have to substitute.

"Where's my fruit?" My daughter looks into her bag, which I threw on the counter.

"It's in the jelly in your sandwich."

"Oh. Can I have some cheese, too?"

"Sure." I rip open a box of macaroni and cheese, grab a package of cheddar flavoring, and quickly toss it into the bag. Then I scrawl: "Princess, do good today. See you soon. Love, Mom."

By Thursday I am definitely no longer bright-eyed or perky and I begin to think it's okay to make a sandwich out of peanut butter and two granola bars because it will cover most of the major food groups and I'm out of bread. Instead, I roll a slice of bologna into a tortilla and toss a lemon into the bag for vitamin C. Then I add a box of Cracker Jacks since popcorn is a vegetable. I grab a piece of paper and quickly write: "Have a great day. Love, Mom. P.S. If the lunchroom monitor sees your lunch, don't give her your real name."

By Friday I invent a fifth food group usually called, "The Mystery Meat Group," and I scrawl a message on the back of my daughter's lunch bag that reads, "To whom it may concern, please believe I am really a good mother." I begin to feel guilty and I wonder if other better-organized mothers sent wonderful culinary creations for their children every day. Maybe sending a homemade lunch to school for my daughter isn't the right thing for me to do.

"Do you want to buy lunch instead?" I ask as I hand her the lunch bag.

"No way! Friday's my favorite lunch day!"

I stare at her blankly.

"I can trade my granola bar for Jimmy's leftover Thursday night pizza. Then, if I add a bag of graham crackers and a box of raisins, I can trade up for Meg's tuna and ketchup sandwich. If I throw in two lemons, I'll have enough for Susie's turkey and mustard salad on a bagel and a bag of chocolate chip cookies."

As I watch her walk down the driveway happily swinging her lunch bag, I remember some of the lunchroom deals I made as a child. Then I realize even though I'm a failure at making lunches like my mother, I'm a success at passing on the art of lunch bag substitution.

Household Tips

Do you ever wonder who makes up all of those do-it-your-self household tips you see in magazines and newspapers? I have a hunch they're invented by the same type of people who clean the slats in their mini blinds, organize their linen closets by color, and whose primary function in life is to make the rest of us look bad. Their motto is, "truly domestically gifted people never need to buy household products"—especially when they can spend more time and money making them at home.

I recently went through a phase where I was brainwashed into believing that even I could make household products that were better, cheaper, and more politically correct than those I could find at the store.

My first creation was a recipe for an all-purpose (and I use this term loosely) cleaning product. The recipe promised to produce a mixture that I could use as a solvent, air freshener, carpet deodorizer and perfume. Armed with nothing but a big metal bucket and limited domestic experience, I poured in the first two ingredients: vodka and tea tree oil. But just as I was beginning to daydream about my sparkling clean tile, I got to the part about adding "lime essential oil" and "grapefruit essential oil" that I had apparently missed before. I was sure I didn't have any—even though I had no idea what "essential oil" was, other than the kind you have to change in the car every three months—so I tossed a capful of orange juice into the bucket instead.

When I was finished, my homemade cleaner smelled more like a cross between dandruff shampoo and a mimosa, and I wasn't sure whether to clean my grout, wash my hair or prepare hors d'oeuvres.

Next, I found a recipe for making homemade deodorant. I'm not sure what intrigued me more, the challenge of having to use a double boiler or the thought of saving three dollars. Nevertheless, I prepared a mold from a recycled toilet paper roll and melted a combination of beeswax, distilled water, rubbing alcohol, cornstarch, and baking soda in the double boiler. When it finally cooled—three hours later—I had a perfect tube of home-made deodorant. Cost: $17.32.

For a while I swore off making anymore household products. Then I read an article about how I could get rid of all of the snails in my garden by setting out pans of beer. According to the author, snails were supposed to be attracted to the beer, slither over for a sip, become intoxicated, then fall head-first into the pan. This seemed plausible since I had seen many of my friends do this in college. But what if it didn't work? I envisioned a band of snails carousing through my garden, trampling my geraniums while doing the limbo, then waking up all the neighbors singing loud, off-key versions of "Louie, Louie" into the early hours of the morning.

I decided to try it anyway because it seemed fast, cheap, and easy. Besides, what did I have to lose? But by the time I had used up my last six pack, my garden didn't look any better, I hadn't found one inebriated snail, and the only living thing actually drinking from the pans of beer was my husband. Once again, I swore off making my own household products.

Then my neighbor, who I suspect is a distant relative of Martha Stewart, brought over a soap recipe that she swore was the best thing since homemade hairspray. And all I needed was nine pounds of animal fat, a cup of borax, some rosin, a can of lye, and a giant vat. I would just have to save up the fat, figure out what the other ingredients were, then melt them together. It could be a nice little project if I had nothing better to do for, say, the next three months.

Instead, I decided to go to the grocery store and buy a bar of bath soap for eighty-nine cents.

It's just easier that way.

The Futile Gourmet

I know the whole issue of food preparation is fairly complex, but I've come to believe that there are two kinds of people in this world: those who don't mind spending hours slaving over a hot stove preparing quality food—and those who prefer eating it. Since my recipe collection consists mostly of foods that can be made with one hand in less than ten minutes, I have a hunch I'm in the latter category. Oh, don't get me wrong, I'd gladly learn to cook properly if there weren't so many other important things to do in the day like, say, finishing crossword puzzles.

I think one of the main problems is that most gourmet cooking terms are too hard to understand. It would be a whole lot easier if there were a little pronunciation key and definition next to each one. For all I know, a "Flambé" is some sort of exotic dance, "Julienne" is the name of the chef's girlfriend, and "Frappé" is how I look on days I wear sweats and don't have time to take a shower. Like most busy, modern women, I prefer my recipes with simple, straightforward directions, such as add water and stir.

It's not that I don't try. I occasionally take all the shoeboxes and wrapping paper out of the oven and make a good home-cooked meal. I can always tell my family is surprised at this by the way they stand around in the kitchen and stare.

"What's that smell?" my daughter asks.

"I'm making a special family recipe for dinner."

"It's not the Cheese Whiz and onion casserole again is it?"

"Don't get smart."

I think the main problem with cooking is that you need to have all the key ingredients stocked in your kitchen at the same time. Believe me; this is harder than it sounds. I'm the type of person who would run out of Cabernet Sauvignon in the middle of making beef tenderloin, substitute with either orange juice or an old wine cooler, and wonder where I went wrong.

I've tried to learn by watching cooking shows on television, but sooner or later I start talking back to the screen. "Yeah, sieving is easy for you to do, lady. You don't have a toddler wrapped around both ankles begging for a blue Popsicle!" Or "Okay, buddy, I'd like to see you 'gently whisk until fluffy' while changing diapers, prying Play Doh out of nostrils, and breaking up fights!" No wonder most television chefs are men—who else would have all that free time to spend in the kitchen?

Then my friend Linda told me about a new type of cooking bag that cooks a main course right in your dishwasher. I could put a whole salmon in it, put it on the top rack next to the coffee mugs, and by the rinse cycle, it would be ready to serve. I'd never have to turn on my oven again, plus I'd have clean dishes. But somehow it just doesn't seem right.

Next my husband told me about a website that would tell me how to make a meal out of the ingredients I already had. Unbelievable as this sounds, all I had to do was type in up to three ingredients and it would suggest recipes I could make the very same night.

After taking a quick inventory, I typed in animal cookies, cheese puffs, and blue popsicles. After a few seconds (and this may come as a big surprise) the site determined that I could make absolutely nothing edible with those ingredients.

So, I tried again. This time I typed in cheese whiz and red onions. A few seconds later, a recipe for Instant Southwestern Cheesy Casserole popped onto the screen. I breathed a sigh of relief. Now that was more like it.

Feng Shui: East Meets Nest

I am sitting on my sofa waiting to feel happy and energized. I know it will happen any minute now since I just spent the day improving my house's feng shui. For those of you lucky enough not to know, feng shui is a popular Chinese interior decorating technique you can use to improve your mood, create power and luck, and increase your energy field.

I decided to try it since I could definitely use the extra energy to keep up with my two children—and the thought of having any kind of power in my life excited me.

According to the book, *The World of Feng Shui*, there are several simple, affordable things you can do to create a gentle, uncomplicated flow of energy, or "chi," throughout your house.

In fact, after only reading the first few pages I found out that the major problem with my house is that the stairway, which points towards the front door, is letting all of my lucky chi run out of the house directly into my yard. Well, let me tell you, while this idea may sound silly at first, it sure explains a lot of things: like why I haven't won the lottery or found a tablecloth that matches my drapery fabric or been able to get rid of all the ants in the kitchen—and why the potted geraniums in front of the house are always doing so well.

The book said that all I would have to do to fix this is to either knock out a wall and point the stairway in a different direction, or slide an object in front of the stairway large enough to block my chi from escaping out the front door and into the house across the street. So I did what any modern woman would do when faced with an interior decorating dilemma: I moved the sofa.

After it was securely in place in front of the stairs, I went into the kitchen where (and this might come as a big surprise to some of you) I saw the refrigerator. This was okay, the book explained, except it would subliminally draw me to it and make me eat more. I would gain weight, become obsessive, turn miserable, and spend my days locked inside the pantry with a gallon of double fudge chocolate ice cream and a box of Twinkies. To think all along I'd been blaming genetics and childbirth for my extra pounds when it was really caused by my misdirected feng shui. I shudder to think about all the money I spent on health club memberships and fad diets when apparently all I needed to do was move my refrigerator out of the kitchen.

But the only empty space near an electrical outlet was in the living room, where the sofa had been. So instead, I decided to disguise the fridge with my children's artwork and move on.

Then chapter two assured me that wind chimes hung in the house would increase my family's creativity. Now I don't know about you, but I'm the type of person who figures if one will do the job, five will do it even better. So I went to the backyard, got my collection of ceramic wind chimes, and placed them in strategic places around the house.

Next I wandered into the bedroom and moved the bed against a solid wall so I would feel safe and secure. Then I moved the mirror away from the foot of the bed so my soul wouldn't rise at night, float to the other side of the room, and be shocked by seeing its own image—although I couldn't imagine this being any different than what I experience walking through a department store during the day.

When I finished with the bedroom, I placed a rug under the computer for its continued good health, placed a clock on the wall across from the office door to subconsciously suggest that anytime is a good time to be there, and put a rock on the book shelf to remind my family of the special association we have with each other, the Earth, and the entire animal kingdom (although, at the moment, I have absolutely no idea what that might be).

And now I'm sitting on the sofa waiting to feel happy, wealthy, energized, and more creative—besides, my back hurts and I have a headache from all of the wind chimes. But I'm not worried. I know feng shui will change my life any minute. I can feel it.

Sew What?

When my daughter received her first Brownie badge, called a "Try-it," I did what any modern woman of the '90's would've done: I congratulated her, then flipped it over to find the adhesive strip so I could attach it onto her uniform sash.

"Mommy, what are you doing?" my daughter said. "You have to sew it on."

Sew it? At first I thought she was kidding. Then real panic set in when I realized she wasn't.

Let me just say that I'm the type of person whose sewing kit consists of a bunch of dull pins, some dental floss, and a stapler. I acquired my only domestic training in the home economics class I was forced to take in high school—because the art classes were full. I spent the entire semester trying to thread the sewing machine and the one time I managed to turn it on, it trapped my sleeves under the bobbin and stitched a seam up my right arm before I could pull the cord out of the wall with my foot.

I had a feeling I was wasting everybody's time—especially the teacher's. According to her, I had absolutely no eye for detail, my stitches were too big, and my fine motor skills were equivalent to that of an inebriated monkey. And that, she implied to my mother, was sugar coating it.

Fifteen years later, I still haven't figured out how to make tiny, even stitches and the last time I saw our sewing machine, it was holding up the back end of my husband's car while he changed a tire.

But I was determined to sew on my daughter's badge. So I spit on my fingertips, closed one eye and threaded the needle. I concentrated and tried to remember how to make a stitch. Any stitch. After several tries I realized that I wasn't dealing with just ordinary embroidered fabric. It was obviously special material made from bulletproof vests. And the name "Try-it" didn't stand for encouragement at all. It was more of a dare aimed at the mothers—as in, "You will never be able to sew this onto your daughter's Brownie sash no matter what you do. Go ahead, sucker, try-it."

About an hour later my eyes were watering and all my important fingers were wrapped in Band-Aids, but I had finally attached the Kevlar patch securely onto the sash. The embroidered triangle was a masterpiece proving beyond all doubt that I was an involved, caring mother. I proudly offered my labor of love to my daughter.

"Mom," she said, "it's upside down."

At first I was just surprised she could make out the design through all the stitches. But when the meaning of her words finally sank in, I did what any intelligent, enlightened mother would do: I denied it.

When she received three more "Try-it's" at her next meeting, I clenched my teeth into a smile and tried to look excited. Then I opened a bottle of glue and slathered it onto the sash.

"What are you doing, Mommy?" my daughter asked.

"Sewing on your patches," I said.

I was impressed with my ingenuity—until the patches started curling up at the corners and falling off. I knew that just as soon as my daughter wore her uniform in public, the word would be out on the street that I was severely domestically challenged, and that it was truly a miracle I'd made it as far along in the world as I had.

But at the next Brownie meeting, I was stunned to find out most of the mothers apparently had the same kind of home economics training I did. One mother had stapled the patches to her daughter's sash while another had used a set of diaper pins. My friend Linda, whom I've always looked upon as the perfect mother, had traced her daughter's patches onto the sash with washable laundry pens.

Suddenly I knew everything would be okay. I didn't even mind when my daughter brought home five new "Try-its" that day. I just did what any modern woman would do: I congratulated her—then went into the garage to find the duct tape.

Pot Luck

I enjoyed taking an active role in my daughter's education until I received a note requesting a donation for the annual classroom International Holiday Feast. I grew suspicious when I noticed it was similar to the lease agreement I signed for my car. At first I was lulled into a false sense of security by the picture of smiling cherubs dancing around a Christmas tree. Then I noticed the words "family project" and "pot luck" farther down the page. Under the line for my signature, the fine print said I had three days to produce my family's favorite dish for my daughter to share in the classroom.

I wanted to create something that would impress the other parents and make my daughter proud, but most of my cooking knowledge came from the back of a Bisquick box. I decided to call my relatives to see if they had any traditional family recipes. After making several calls, I realized my defective cooking gene was inherited. Instead of getting instructions on how to create a customary dish, I got directions for microwaving TV dinners, advice for making Minute Rice that doesn't stick to the pan, and the number of a local Chinese take-out service.

I sat down at the kitchen table and began to plan our international cuisine. "We need to make something based on our family traditions," I said. "Something exotic and impressive."

"Like macaroni and cheese?" my daughter asked.

I shook my head. Then I remembered the *Domestic Goddess Culinary Cookbook* I'd stored in the back of the closet when I became a mother of two. I pulled it out and skimmed through the pages.

"This is perfect." I pointed to a picture of a cream cheese igloo, surrounded by a pack of penguins made from olives and carrot wedges skewered on a toothpick. "It's called Penguin Paradise."

It was neither international nor traditional, but it was impressive, and I figured it wouldn't be too hard to make since cream cheese is close in texture to Play-Doh.

We went to the grocery store to buy the ingredients: eight boxes of cream cheese, five cans of olives, two carrots, and a box of toothpicks. As I stood in line, I started having flashbacks of my first pregnancy. Then I noticed a woman behind me with twelve boxes of cheese balls, five boxes of raisins, and a bag of marshmallows.

"Cheese ball snowmen with ear muffs and ski hats," she said, "and you?"

"A cream cheese igloo and enough penguins to feed thirty-two kindergartners for a week."

She nodded knowingly.

When we arrived home, we began to assemble our masterpiece. I worked on molding the cream cheese into an igloo while my daughter carefully made the penguins.

She poked a toothpick through two olives then added carrot wedges for the beak and feet. When we finished, we had created a work of art: a Picasso. Several penguins had beaks sticking into their stomachs and carrot feet on their heads.

The igloo looked like a large, yawning, white turtle.

"We did it," my daughter said holding up a penguin. "Just like the picture!"

I didn't have the heart to fix it.

The next morning I brought our contribution to school and put it on the back table before any of the other parents spotted it. As my daughter sat on the carpet with the other children, I looked at the other culinary creations: a tray of lopsided cheese ball snowmen in ski hats, a wreath made by pouring macaroni and cheese into a Jell-O mold, three dozen store-bought cupcakes, and a fruitcake still in the tin. I was relieved to find no sign of traditional family recipes anywhere.

I proudly slid our tray into the center of the table. "It's not so bad after all," I thought as a group of children gathered around it.

"Hey, look!" a little boy said, pointing to the igloo. "A big, white turtle."

He reached over and flung an olive into the opening. "Cool."

Our creation was a success.

$\mathcal{S}$pring Over-Organization Syndrome

Spring isn't just about pastel colors, blooming flowers and baby birds. Noooo. In fact, spring brings on all kinds of peculiar conditions. First there's spring fever, which causes normally responsible people to sleep in late, skip classes and shirk going to work just so they can take a walk in the park and feel the sun on their faces. Then there's the typical colds and flu. And I don't even have to mention the allergies. But there's one condition no one ever warns you about: Over-Organization Syndrome.

Yes, it's true. It's as if every spring I'm suddenly infused with energy and flooded with ambition to fling aside my flannel robe and fuzzy slippers and pick up everything that's been laying on the floor since last winter.

Now some of you are probably thinking, "So what? That's not so bad. I mean we could all use a little more organization in our lives, you know?" And, of course, you're right. But the problem is, once you start, things can quickly get out of control. One minute you'll find yourself leisurely color-coding the bath towels in the linen closet and the next, your standing over the Barbie Beach House sorting miniature shoes by color and heel height.

No one knows what causes this. Some people might chalk it up to a natural desire for renewal. More spiritual people might think of it as some kind of a supernatural experience. Me, I blame it on allergy medication.

Take the other day, for example. I woke up thinking, "Gee, I really should pack up the kid's winter clothes."

So I started sorting them. But it didn't stop there. After that I took down the curtains to wash them and put fresh sheets on the beds. By lunchtime I'd moved on to the bookcase where I spent the rest of the afternoon putting the books into alphabetical order. Then before I knew it, I'd started in on the kitchen junk drawer. The rest of the day was a blur.

Oh sure, you're probably thinking, I could've stopped myself. But past experience has taught me that once you've caught

Over-Organization Syndrome, it's best to just go along with it and let it run its course.

And believe it or not, there will come a day when you'll suddenly take a look around and realize that you've now become an Officially Organized Person. You not only have all of the spices alphabetized and the wrapping paper in order, you're among the elite who have Legos stored in matching plastic containers—separated by color.

Of course, one of the big drawbacks to being so organized is that you can no longer find anything when you need it. One day last April it took us over two hours to find a pad of paper and a pen. We looked in all of the usual places, like behind the entertainment center and on the floorboards in the back seat of the car. We finally found it by accident, lying in the top desk drawer, *exactly where it belonged.*

The other drawback is that your title as an Officially Organized Person never lasts longer than two months. Three tops. Just when you're getting used to it, the urge to organize goes away. And by midsummer the Hot Wheels cars are back in the planter, the car keys are again dangling from the top of the TV antenna, and sorting anything by color becomes a laughable idea.

I tell you, it's a funny thing how nature works.

Kitchen Remodeling

You will not believe what happened to my friend Karen: she has a bad case of Home Improvement Run Amok.

For those of you who don't know what this is, it's a mysterious condition that mainly strikes property owners, compelling them to suddenly give gobs of money to contractors, redecorators, or professional landscapers for no apparent reason.

Let me explain. It all started when Karen set out to replace a light bulb in her refrigerator. It was the fifth bulb to go out in a month and she began to think that perhaps something was wrong with the refrigerator. So she decided it was time for a new one.

Now, this was all fine and good and it should've been the end of the story except when the new refrigerator arrived, it refused to fit into its allotted space in the kitchen.

So instead of returning it Karen did the next best thing: she replaced all of her cabinets with taller ones. But that's not all. After the cabinets were installed, the linoleum floor looked dingy, so she replaced it with tile. And, then, of course, the counter tops needed to be upgraded to match the floor. Before she knew it, she'd put over $15,000 into a kitchen that didn't needed replacing.

This, my friends, is an example of the dreaded, Home Improvements Run Amok disease.

So what Karen wanted to know from me is at what point she was supposed to stop.

"Tell me what happened," she said. "I mean, where was the signal?"

Frankly, I don't know why she's asking me. As a person who's never made any kind of home improvement (except, perhaps, changing the furnace filter), I must admit her story gave me the chills.

In fact, it still haunted me three weeks later when I told my friend Linda about it.

"Oh, relax," she said. "This kind of thing happens all the time." And she went on to tell me about how just a few weeks earlier, she'd bought a new bedspread that didn't exactly match the curtains. So she took them down and put up mini blinds instead. This, of course, looked nice, except that now the walls needed to be painted to brighten up the rest of the room. When she'd finished, she somehow noticed that among all this bright fresh paint, her clothes didn't look all that great anymore. So now she's in the process of replacing her entire wardrobe, one piece at a time!

Astonishing! But the fact of the matter is, anyone can catch a case of Home Improvement Run Amok if they're not careful.

Like last week, for example, when I innocently decided to paint the front door. Sure enough, before I knew it I'd moved on to the side of the house and was painting full steam ahead towards the garage. And don't bother asking me why. All I know is that I was just contemplating whether or not to hire someone to touch up the eaves or get a ladder and do it myself when my husband wrestled the brush out of my hands and made me go inside.

And to think that he didn't even listen to me when I explained to him that there's absolutely nothing wrong with a little fresh paint. After all, it's human nature to want change. Right? RIGHT?

Yes, it's a funny thing how the mind works. If you ask most homeowners, they'll tell you that the only way to prevent Home Improvement Run Amok disease is to set firm limits and stick to them.

Which makes a lot of sense. So that's what I'm going to do from now on.

That and, oh yeah, keep lots of extra light bulbs on hand for the refrigerator.

Just for the Record

There are radical changes going on at my house: you can now get into the upstairs bathroom by going through my bedroom closet.

Let me explain.

Some time last week the caulking in the shower got tired of being taken for granted and decided to, what the heck, let all of the water seep out through the wall and into, you guessed it, the closet.

Once I was over the shock of my carpet and entire wardrobe being wet, I did what any naïve, panic-stricken person would do: I called my friendly home insurance company.

Now I want to stop here for a minute and say that I have nothing against insurance companies. In fact, mine has always been embarrassingly generous with things like maps and colorful stickers and theme park discounts.

When I called them, they seemed very glad to hear from me. They listened sympathetically while I told them all about the water and the caulking and the fate of my cardboard shoetree. When I finished, they gently assured me that "an adjuster" would get back to me as soon as possible to handle my claim.

I hung up the phone fantasizing about teams of eager workman rapidly repairing my upstairs closet and laying my brand new, top of the line, off-white, plush Berber carpet.

Then I called my friend Julie to tell her my good news.

"You did WHAT?" she exclaimed. "Everybody knows that you can't report claims to your insurance company. What were you thinking?"

"Well, I . . ."

"Now you'll have a *record*," she went on. "You'll have a high risk house."

Everyone knows that having a record is something not to be taken lightly. I mean, bad drivers have records. Convicted felons have records. Now, apparently, even houses that are standing still minding their own business have records.

And don't think for a minute that you can keep it a secret. For years, possibly centuries, prospective homebuyers, strangers, and nosey insurance companies will be able to access your house's record and find out exactly what kind of shoddy dump you're running. And it's not like you can go off one morning to a special Negligent Home Owners' School and get your transgression removed, either.

Call me naïve, but I still had some hope left when the insurance adjuster, I'll call her Janice, came to my house to survey the damage. I took her upstairs and pointed to the giant hole in the back of my closet, which my husband created while trying to find the source of the leak.

Our conversation went something like this:

Me: "I was thinking of a new carpet in Berber preferably something in a beige."

Janice: "That sounds nice, but the carpet isn't covered."

Me: "Oh. Okay, how about the wall then?"

Janice: "Nope."

Me: "The floor?"

Janice: "No."

Me: "The caulking? The paint? My shoetree?"

Janice: "Uh, no."

"What, exactly *is* covered then?" I finally asked.

"Well, fire damage is covered," she said brightly, and I thought I heard her add, "but only if it's started on a Tuesday by a group of feral squirrels accidentally rubbing two sticks and a walnut together." (But I could've imagined this last part.)

I admit, a part of me wanted to grab Janice by her lapel and launch into a diatribe about my stellar record of on-time premium payments, the misleading piles of free maps, and the cheery bumper stickers.

But all that came out was, "I . . . I thought you cared!"

And I'm sure on some level she did. But instead of showing it, she rolled her eyes in an "of course" sort of way and said, "We can't possibly cover everything, you know."

I admit, from a certain business standpoint, it did make sense.

So I wasn't too surprised when she called me a few days later, as promised, with the bad news: by the time I paid the carpet layer, the cleaner and the various inspectors, I would end up owing the insurance company about five hundred dollars. And on top of all that, there'd be a record.

That said, we no longer have a hole in the back of the bedroom closet, rather we have a custom second entrance into the bathroom. An inadvertent home improvement.

That's my story, and I'm sticking to it.

HOLLiDAYS ARE THE MOST WONDERFUL TiME OF YEAR
(AND OTHER FANTiSiES)

A Mother's Letter to Santa

Dear Santa,

I've been a good mom all year. I've fed, cleaned, and cuddled my two children on demand, visited the doctor's office more than my doctor, sold sixty-two cases of candy bars to raise money to plant a shade tree in the school playground, and figured out how to attach nine patches onto my daughter's girl scout sash with staples and a glue gun.

I was hoping you could spread my list out over several Christmases, since I had to write this one with my son's red crayon on the back of a receipt in the laundry room between cycles, and who knows when I'll find any more free time in the next eighteen years.

Here are my Christmas wishes:

I'd like a pair of legs that don't ache after a day of chasing kids (in any color, except purple, which I already have) and arms that don't flap in the breeze, but are strong enough to carry a screaming toddler out of the candy aisle in the grocery store. I'd also like a waist, since I lost mine somewhere in the seventh month of my last pregnancy.

If you're hauling big ticket items this year, I'd like a car with fingerprint resistant windows and a radio that only plays adult music; a television that doesn't broadcast any programs containing talking animals; and a refrigerator with a secret compartment behind the crisper where I can hide to talk on the phone.

On the practical side, I could use a talking daughter doll that says, "Yes, Mommy" to boost my parental confidence, along with one potty-trained toddler, two kids who don't fight, and three pairs of jeans that zip all the way up without the use of power tools. I could also use a recording of Tibetan monks chanting, "Don't eat in the living room," and "Take your hands off your brother," because my voice seems to be out of my children's hearing range and can only be heard by dogs. And please, don't forget the Play-Doh Travel Pack, the hottest stocking stuffer this year for mothers of preschoolers. It comes in three fluorescent colors guaranteed to crumble on any carpet and make the in-laws' house seem just like home.

If it's too late to find any of these products, I'd settle for enough time to brush my teeth and comb my hair in the same morning, or the luxury of eating food warmer than room temperature without it being served in a Styrofoam container.

If you don't mind, I could also use a few Christmas miracles to brighten the holiday season. Would it be too much trouble to declare ketchup a vegetable? It will clear my conscience immensely. It would be helpful if you could coerce my children to help around the house without demanding payment as if they were the bosses of an organized crime family; or if my toddler didn't look so cute sneaking downstairs to eat contraband ice cream in his pajamas at midnight.

Well, Santa, the buzzer on the dryer is ringing and my son saw my feet under the laundry room door and wants his crayon back. Have a safe trip, and remember to leave your wet boots by the chimney and come in and dry off by the fire so you don't catch cold. Help yourself to cookies on the table, but don't eat too many or leave crumbs on the carpet.

Always,
Mom

P.S. One more thing Santa, you can cancel all my requests if you can keep my children young enough to believe in you.

$\mathcal{M}$y Halloween Angel

The scariest holiday at my house is Halloween. From the first week of October, I live in sheer terror of my young daughter asking for a homemade costume. Ghosts, ghouls, and goblins are nothing compared to facing the electric torture device called the sewing machine. In fact, the last time I used one was somewhere between the decline of the disco era and the Reagan years.

"I want to be a fairy princess!" my daughter announced. "Like Cinderella."

"How about a ghost," I pleaded, "or something else with one seam?"

"A princess," she insisted, "with lace, puffy sleeves, and lots of jewels!"

I silently cursed the other mothers on the block who diligently sewed their children's costumes each year. During the month of October, the street was filled with the hum of sewing machines coming from every direction—except my house.

"Buy a costume at the mall," my husband said. "Why go to all that trouble?"

"It's a labor of love," I explained, "like having a homemade cake at your birthday party instead of a grocery store special."

"Remember last year," he continued, "when you used the stapler and her halo kept poking the back of her head and her angel wings blew off into the gutter?"

"She looked very cute while it lasted, I said, "and I enjoyed creating the costume," I paused, "but I just don't have the time for sewing." I drummed my fingers on the counter and bit my lower lip. Then I realized I still had the angel gown upstairs in my daughter's closet.

The next day I dyed the white cloth pink in the bathtub and closed the wing holes with masking tape. I added lace to the front with a glue gun and stuffed the shoulders with tissue. Then I trimmed last year's halo down to a tiara and sprinkled a stick from the backyard with glitter for a magic wand. I carefully hung my creation on the top rack of my daughter's closet hoping everything would stick.

On Halloween eve I carefully taped my daughter into her costume.

"I'm beautiful!" she twirled in front of the hall mirror.

"Just like Cinderella?" I asked.

"No," she paused, "just like you." She kissed me on the cheek.

I promised my husband I would hand out candy this year while he chaperoned the trick or treating. As I watched them go down the front walk, I saw the lace begin to peel, two strips of masking tape blowing in the wind, and a wad of tissue working its way out of the right sleeve—but my daughter was smiling and happily waving her wand. Although she looked like Cinderella, she will always be my little angel underneath. She turned and blew me a kiss from halfway down the street and I waved back, knowing the reason I went through all that trouble.

Making the Cut

This Halloween my five-year-old son insisted on having a dinosaur carved into the side of his pumpkin. Now maybe it's me, but I've noticed that pumpkin carving sure isn't what it used to be. Only a few years ago a respectable jack-o'-lantern had two triangle eyes, a tiny triangle nose, and a jaunty crescent mouth with a crooked tooth. The only complicated part was deciding which pumpkin to take home from the patch.

Recently, however, pumpkin carving has become an art form of its own that requires all the skill and precision of say, brain surgery. I'm not sure how this happened. It might be because people were tired of looking at the same old jack-o-lantern year after year. Or perhaps it's the result of a marketing conspiracy. But my theory, and frankly I can't get anyone to back this up, is that one day the overzealous, crafty people of the world got together and started carving things like witches, ghosts, and mummies onto the fronts of pumpkins while all of the un-crafty people in the world weren't looking. And now you can hardly pass a house on Halloween night without seeing a jack-o-lantern with an intricate work of art on its front.

Now, since I'm the type of person who has trouble cutting a sandwich into two equal parts, you'd think my son would know better than to ask me to carve a dinosaur onto a pumpkin. You would think.

"Don't worry," my friend Julie said. "All you need to do is go to the grocery store and get one of those carving kits with patterns and tools in it."

Of course this sounded like reasonable advice. But when I went to the store, I couldn't find a dinosaur kit anywhere. In fact, I wondered if there was such a thing at all. Either that or all of the un-artistic, desperate parents in this town got there before me.

So instead I bought a kit for a hunched backed cat and decided to improvise.

When we got home my son and I cleaned out the pumpkin and spread out the miniature carving tools on the kitchen table.

Then I scanned the directions, taped the pattern onto the pumpkin, drew a few dinosaur-like spikes onto the tail, and began making pinpoint holes along the pattern with the special poker tool.

I must admit things were going surprisingly well. Then it was time to rip the pattern off the pumpkin and start cutting.

I decided to start at the top and work down—which any fool would know is a better plan for, say, washing windows than carving a dinosaur onto a pumpkin.

I quickly found out, as surprising as this may seem, that it is impossible to make any kind of a precision cut with a saw the size of a nail file. At first I pushed too hard and nicked off the corner of a spike. Next I pushed too gently and couldn't cut at all. And then, just when I discovered the optimum cutting pressure and thought all of my problems were solved, the saw hit a slick spot, veered off to the left, and chopped off the dinosaur's head.

"Mom, you're not doing it right," my son said.

Now granted this set things back a bit, so I did the only thing I could think of: I reattached the head by jabbing a couple of red frilly cocktail toothpicks through it. This worked so well, in fact, that I used a blue one to reattach the spike and three more yellow ones to reinforce the tail.

As great as this idea seemed at first, by the time we were finished the pumpkin looked more like a piña colada than a dinosaur.

I held it out to my son anyway, and he considered it silently for a moment.

"Cool," he said finally. "A space alien!"

I just smiled and set it on the front porch. And although we had the most interesting pumpkin on the block, a part of me longed for the good old days, back when we had old-fashioned jack-o'-lanterns with triangle eyes and jaunty crescent mouths.

Life was so much simpler then.

Thanksgiving Leftovers

Let's face it. The most distinguishable trait about Thanksgiving isn't the football game, the parade, or the quality time you get to spend with your relatives—it's the leftovers.

Oh, don't start yelling. I know what the true meaning of Thanksgiving is just as well as anybody else. Any fool will tell you it's a day for people to open their hearts and homes, reflect, and give thanks for their good fortune and all that. But let's be fair here. Without Thanksgiving there would be no need for you to spend an entire day in the kitchen wrestling with a temperamental piecrust and an unreliable turkey baster. And I bet those of you who have (and you know who you are) will agree with me that leftovers are a synonym of freedom. The problem is figuring out how to get rid of them.

For example I, being an avid non-cooker, try to get as many meals out of them as scientifically possible. Unfortunately, this is not as easy as you would think. Oh, I know there are some families who actually eat leftovers willingly but believe me, once the word is out at my house that the homemade casserole I served for dinner is really three-day-old diced sweet potatoes and stuffing covered in cheese sauce, my non-cooking days are over. Yes-sir-ee.

However, if my past experience dealing with Thanksgiving leftovers has taught me anything at all, it's that I can get away with serving cranberry and turkey sandwiches once, maybe twice, before my family starts to catch on and I must use all of my wits to outsmart them.

My friend Julie is good at this. Each year her family unknowingly eats a variation of Thanksgiving dinner for every meal well into December. This is because on the day after the holiday she serves them a huge dinner of cold turkey, stuffing, and everything else she had saved from the night before. Then, sometime during dessert, she wanders into the kitchen, opens the refrigerator door, throws her arms out to her sides and loudly proclaims, "Oh my! I can't *believe* the leftovers are all gone already!" And her family never suspects a thing.

Of course it would be ridiculous to assume that something this easy would work with my family. Mainly because they know me too well. So, life being what it is, in order to get rid of my leftovers I must become a master of disguise. Over the years I've tried everything from turning the string bean casserole into soup, to mixing yams with mashed potatoes, to hiding cranberry sauce underneath lettuce in the salad. Last year, in one particularly desperate moment, I trimmed handfuls of stuffing into fun shapes with cookie cutters.

As shocking as it seems, it's not just me. My friend Linda, who is an abnormally creative cook, gets rid of her leftovers by serving bizarre dishes like spaghetti turkey pie and Tex Mex turkey pizza. And my friend Teri makes a convincing sweet potato quiche. But this somehow just seems wrong.

I bet by now you're probably thinking that it would be a lot easier to just toss the leftovers in the garbage can or feed them to the dog. And, you're right.

However, I'm going to celebrate by stocking up on plastic wrap and tin foil. Call it what you will, but, in the words of my friend Julie: a Thanksgiving without leftovers is just no Thanksgiving at all.

What a Mother is Thankful For

I never intended to tell you anything about this, but since I became an adult I discovered that the meaning of Thanksgiving sure isn't what it used to be. When I was younger, I remember receiving the inevitable homework assignment to write an essay on "something I am thankful for." Then I'd spend a lot of time sitting in my room trying to figure out just what in the world that could possibly be, and I'd end up writing down everything I could think of from God to environmental consciousness.

But after having children, my priorities have clearly changed.

Before children: I was thankful to have been born in the United States of America—the most powerful, free, democracy in the world.

After children: I am thankful for Velcro tennis shoes. As well as saving valuable time, now I can hear the sound of my son taking off his shoes—which gives me three extra seconds to activate the safety locks on the backseat windows right before he hurls them out of the car and onto the freeway.

Before children: I was thankful for the recycling program that will preserve our natural resources and prevent the overflowing of landfills.

After children: I am thankful for swim diapers because every time my son wanders into water in plain disposables, he ends up wearing a blimp the size of, say, New Jersey, on his bottom.

Before children: I was thankful for fresh, organic vegetables.

After children: I am thankful for microwavable macaroni and cheese—without which my children would be surviving on about three bites of cereal and their own spit.

Before children: I was thankful for the opportunity to obtain a college education and have a higher quality of life than my ancestors.

After children: I am thankful to finish a complete thought without being interrupted.

Before children: I was thankful for holistic medicine and natural herbs.

After children: I am thankful for any pediatric cough syrup guaranteed to

"cause drowsiness" in young children.

Before children: I was thankful for all of the teachers who had taught, encouraged, and nurtured me throughout my formative years.

After children: I am thankful for all of the people at Weight Watchers who let me strip down to pantyhose and a strategically placed scarf before getting on the scale each week.

Before children: I was thankful for the opportunity to vacation in exotic foreign countries so I could experience a different way of life in a new culture.

After children: I am thankful to have time to make it all the way down the driveway to get the mail.

Before children: I was thankful for the Moosewood Vegetarian Cookbook.

After children: I am thankful for the Butterball turkey hotline.

Before children: I was thankful for a warm, cozy home to share with my loved ones.

After children: I am thankful for the lock on the bathroom door.

Before children: I was thankful for material objects like custom furniture, a nice car, and trendy clothes.

After children: I am thankful when the baby spits up and misses my good shoes.

Before children: I was thankful for my wonderful family.

After children: I am thankful for my wonderful family.

☆ Mother's Valentine

This year for Valentine's Day, instead of giving my children another stale bag of candy hearts, I decided to sit down and write each one a love note that contained all of the special things I was always too tired, or too busy, to say.

Dearest Daughter,

You gave me my first experience of motherhood, immortality, and natural childbirth. You gave me my figure back from hours of walking up and down the hallway as you screamed and I wore out a set of tires on the new family car driving you around until you fell asleep. I made you wear the fleece snowsuit with feet you hated so you would stay warm; and I changed your diaper, while you shivered in the cold and dark at 3:00 a.m., so you wouldn't be sore the next day. I locked the refrigerator so you wouldn't eat cookies for breakfast and I tortured you by serving green vegetables with your dinner.

I had the nerve to pull you away from your favorite TV program to make you run and play outside with the neighborhood children in the fresh air—and the gall to make you stay in the house when it rained.

I loved you even when you put my expensive lipstick on the cat and tried dressing your little brother in my good negligee. I loved you through your "me" phase, your "sensitive" phase, and the "only eat purple things" phase. I learned how to mix red and blue dye just right so you would eat more than lollipops and Jell-O.

The ballet lessons you cried through weren't punishment, but my gift of grace and art to you, so you'd grow up to be a well-rounded young lady. And all my good-bye kisses before school, in front of your sophisticated kindergarten friends, were never meant to embarrass you—they were to comfort me.

I never meant to torture you by scrubbing your face and forcing you into your best clothes just to smile in front of a camera. I just wanted memories of what a wonderful child you are.

I love you always,
Mom

P.S. I wasn't really going to sell you to the Gypsies for a dollar if you told my age and weight to your Kindergarten class on sharing day.

Dearest Son,

You are truly special. Being my youngest child, you gave me renewed energy, confidence, and a second chance to ask for an epidural. I let you cry a little longer in your crib and I discovered diaper lotion would protect your bottom through the night. I realized you would survive if you ate an occasional cookie for breakfast and your brain wouldn't shrivel if you watched three Barney videos in a row so I could take a shower and do the laundry.

I loved you even when you used my good china for home plate, and put the snails you found sitting on the driveway in the microwave to warm them up because they looked "cold." I loved you through your clingy stage, your independent stage, and your "wear nothing but boots" stage, although I still have trouble explaining that year's Christmas picture. I was proud you were such a good sport when I was too late to sign you up for soccer practice and you ended up being the only boy in ballet class, and when you held my hand on your first day of preschool when I couldn't stop crying.

I didn't mean to miss brushing your teeth on nights I was too tired to squeeze the toothpaste out of the tube or to embarrass you by making you wear a coat over your diaper and Superman cape when you went out to play in the rain. I really meant to take more pictures so your baby album wouldn't go straight from birth to preschool graduation, but our time together went too fast.

I love you always,
Mom

P.S. I really wasn't going to trade you for a poodle the time you put your bug collection in the crisper to eat the lettuce. I wouldn't have traded you for the world.

When I finished writing, I realized my children were too young to understand what my valentines meant, so I slipped each one into their scrapbooks to wait patiently until they became parents, too.

Mother's Bill of Rights

This Fourth of July, I reflected on the days when I used to have independence. Since the birth of my two children, the only freedom I get is when I hide in the laundry room, on top of the dryer. I decided the Constitution, a model for human rights and democracy, gives little hope to mothers who don't have time to pursue life or liberty, and whose happiness is stopping at a red light to finish brushing their teeth in the rear view mirror. Someone has to uphold the rights of a group of people whose arms are too tired by the end of the day to hold up anything.

The Mother's Bill of Rights

Article I: A Mom has the right to freedom of speech. She may talk on the phone during the day (and finish a conversation) without having to see a circus side show put on by her children consisting of invisible wounds, lost ladybugs, and a gymnastics routine using the sofa and halogen lamp.

Article II: Mom has the right to confiscate any inanimate object used as a weapon, including the television remote or anything found underneath the sofa cushion. Gymnastic Barbie may not be bent into a slingshot and used to pelt unsuspecting siblings with tiny stiletto heels.

Article III: All mothers have the natural right to bear and utilize one of the most dangerous and powerful weapons in the world: guilt.

Article IV: Moms have the right to peacefully assemble. Once a week mothers will meet a group of friends for a leisurely meal they don't have to cook—while the children stay home with Dad.

Article V: Mom has the right not to be a victim of cruel and unusual punishment. No Mom is required to sit through a movie containing talking animals more than once and no one is to climb into her bed before 7:00 a.m., take all the covers, and warm their cold feet on her back.

Article VI: Mom has the right to own unbroken possessions that don't cook, clean or vacuum. No one may enter her room without consent, use her expensive lipstick to draw a hopscotch on the sidewalk, or try to sell the good crystal from a booth in the driveway for a dollar.

Article VII: Mothers have the right to bestow wisdom, such as: a public toilet that looks clean is dirty, and a sippy cup that looks dirty is clean.

Article VIII: Mothers have the right to donate any toy left on the kitchen floor to charity, or string it on fishing line and turn it into a Christmas ornament.

Article IX: Mothers have the right to vigorously promote coats and vegetables. Children caught catapulting corn across the dining room with a fork instead of eating it or playing in the rain without a jacket will be severely punished by Article III.

Article X: Mothers have the right to prohibit anyone under five from asking, "But, why?" before their first cup of coffee.

Amendment I: A mother has the right to love her children unconditionally—forever.

Easter Basket Case

I love Easter morning. It's the only time my children look below their knees and actually bend over to pick something up. I usually spend days boiling, dying, and hiding dozens of eggs around the house under various pieces of furniture. Unfortunately, my children's excitement wears off shortly after retrieving them.

This year I wanted to try a new activity where I didn't have to eat "nature's perfect food" for every meal until Memorial Day. So I looked for this month's edition of *The Perfect Parent* that I'd stuffed into the oven along with the extra shoeboxes and junk mail. I found it and quickly turned to the holiday tips section, hoping to get some creative ideas for a family Easter experience.

The first article suggested piercing raw Easter egg shells with a pin, blowing out the inside and painting miniature spring scenes with a Q-tip inside of the hollow shell. I ruled out this idea since all of my pins were holding seams together and we hadn't bought Q-tips since the time my son inserted them into his nostrils and wouldn't stop barking like a walrus.

I kept turning the pages until I found the "Fast, Easy, and Fun" section for un-artistic, tired parents.

A short article suggested filling plastic eggs with special messages and jellybeans. A picture of a smiling family, joyously ripping open plastic eggs and reading tiny, uplifting messages accompanied it. It was perfect.

The night before Easter, I waited until my children went to bed then I cut strips of paper and spread out a dozen multi-colored eggs on the kitchen table. The article suggested I write "wise, warm, and encouraging" messages. I thought carefully for a moment then wrote: "You are very special," "You make me proud," and "I love you." I slipped the notes into the eggs with a few jellybeans. I couldn't wait until my children found them tomorrow morning.

I quickly opened four more eggs. My pen hovered over the paper for a moment, then I printed, "You are bright" and "Always do your best." I put the strips inside and stared at the remaining slips of paper. I tapped my pen on the table then slowly wrote: "Use your own toothbrush," and "Don't spit on your brother." I stuffed them into an egg with extra jellybeans.

I spent ten minutes trying to think of more wise messages to bestow on my children. After fixing a cup of coffee, alphabetizing my canned vegetables, and cleaning the lint out of the dryer all I could come up with was: "You will prosper," and "Your lucky numbers are 2, 14, and 7."

I quickly filled the rest of the eggs with jellybeans and hid them around the house so I could get some sleep before tomorrow morning.

The next day my children were excited as I handed them their baskets.

"The Easter Bunny left colored eggs this year with special surprises," I said.

Within seconds I heard a squeal of delight coming from behind the sofa. My daughter had found an egg. She opened it, tossed the message on the floor, and popped the jellybeans into her mouth.

My three-year-old son returned chewing on a piece of paper. His basket contained popcorn kernels, two plastic eggs, and a wad of fuzzy gum.

"What a waste of time," I thought. "It would've been more efficient if I'd filled the laundry basket with Easter grass and dyed their socks."

Then my daughter picked up her discarded message off the floor.

"What does it say?" she asked.

"I love you."

"Oh." She walked over and handed it to her brother.

I felt proud of my daughter, and proud of myself for helping to create this moment.

He considered it for a moment, then took the piece of paper, and tossed it into his mouth.

"It's not for eating," my daughter cried. "It's for keeping." Even though I had to pry open his jaw and fish the paper out with my fingers, I knew the Easter experiment wasn't a complete waste of time after all.

*M*other's New Year Resolutions

I always start the New Year by writing a list of ambitious resolutions that are harder to achieve than fitting into my pre-pregnancy jeans. Although I always start out with the best of intentions, this year I figure I might be more successful if I lower my standards and modify my resolutions to reach more reasonable goals.

Last year's resolution: The television will remain off during school days. Quality family time will be spent reading, talking to each other, exploring the outdoors, or doing arts and crafts.

This year's resolution: The television will remain off every other Tuesday morning on even months beginning with the letter "J." We will spend quality time eating fast food out of Styrofoam containers and seeing who can make the fanciest design in catsup with their fries.

Last year: I will create gourmet meals from scratch, seasoned with fresh herbs from my garden.

This year: I will use a spice other than salt.

Last year: I will decorate my house with custom holiday items handmade from dried cuttings grown in my backyard.

This year: I will make a homemade Christmas wreath for the PTA potluck by pouring macaroni and cheese into a Jell-O mold.

Last year: I will improve my mind by joining a local book club so I can read and have lively discussions on current literature.

This year: I will stay awake long enough to read a picture book to my children without falling asleep in their beds.

Last year: I will take time to talk and actively listen to my children so I can learn about who they are and grow to respect them as individuals.

This year: I will not nod off when my daughter tells me what she did at school, who she ate lunch with, how much she ate, how much everybody else ate, the rules of the new game she played at recess, how many times she won, and the plot of the last Disney movie she watched—even if my brain goes numb and my teeth fall asleep.

Last year: I will strive to lose weight and be more organized and successful, like my childless friends.

This year: I will make my childless friends feel overweight, disorganized, and inadequate by having them baby-sit my children.

Last year: I will try to stay informed on political happenings and current events.

This year: I will try to remember what day it is, where I live and my real name.

Last Year: I will make my children's Halloween costumes, entire school wardrobe, and a set of custom curtains for their bedroom that match the Disney characters on their wallpaper.

This year: I will attach my daughter's Girl Scout patches without using a glue gun and stapler.

Last year: I will let my children know how much I love them.

This year: I will let my children know how much I love them.

When I finished writing I stuck the list on the refrigerator and as I popped a bag of frozen peas into the microwave and hid a basket of ironing behind the sofa, I knew I had finally made some resolutions I could keep.

Really, You Shouldn't Have

I'm not sure why this happens, but no matter how many hours I shop at the mall or how much money I spend on Christmas gifts, I'm always one present short.

Now, deep down, I know that the true meaning of the season is about love and good will towards man and all that, but I can't help feeling bad when all of my shopping is done and some well-meaning person (for whom I never once thought of buying something) comes along and gives me a gift. And not just any gift, mind you, it's usually something in the range of jewelry or pricey perfume. Oh, it's not like I'm ungrateful, but whenever this happens I'm left with two options: either admitting that I am, indeed, an uncaring, thoughtless sort of person or saying, "Merry Christmas! Here's *your* present!" then handing them the first box I can grab out from underneath the tree.

Let me just say that either option can get you into a lot of trouble. For example, one Christmas Eve my neighbor Sue unexpectedly came over and gave me a bottle of French cologne while I, after frantically rooting around under the tree, handed her a nicely wrapped box containing a pair of men's socks.

After that, of course, I vowed to plan better, but the problem with unexpected gifts is that there's just no telling who they might be from. The following year I had a bottle of Channel No. 5 ready for Sue. But did she bring me anything? Noooo. Instead I received a hand-carved sculpture of a wooden bear from our neighbor Sam who, I quickly found out, had absolutely no use for expensive perfume.

Then there was the time I tried outwitting surprise gift-givers by buying five extra Christmas baskets, filled with assorted cheeses and decorated with cheery little snowman in jaunty red caps. I lined them up under the tree and looked forward to handing them out with a flourish of *je ne sais quoi*. Of course, life being what it is, this not only prevented me from being a gift short, it also guaranteed that I wouldn't receive any extra presents at all that year and my family would be stuck eating cheese for every meal until September.

And I'm not the only one who's caught off guard by unplanned gifts. Once I gave an art deco wall clock to a close friend who lives down the street. It circulated to four other houses around the neighborhood before mysteriously ending up, freshly wrapped, back under our tree.

However, things could always be worse. For instance, I could be the last minute recipient of several llama-shaped Chia pets or I could panic, like my friend Sandy did, and accidentally give a wrapped CD player to an acquaintance I only meet for lunch twice a year. This just goes to show that until December 26, no one is safe.

So this year I did the only thing I could think of to make Christmas work out even: I bought gifts for everyone I know. Then I delivered them first.

But, I admit, as great as this idea sounds, I didn't really think it all the way through.

And I guess I shouldn't have been too surprised when I received in return a set of personalized golf balls with the initials T.C. on the side, a bar of hotel soap, and a dancing hula doll left over from my neighbor's summer trip to Hawaii.

Ah, well. But between you and me, at least this time if anyone surprises me with an unexpected Christmas gift or two, I'll be ready.

Halloween:
The Kick Off of the Holiday Candy Season

I didn't want to tell you this, but the fact of the matter is I dread Halloween. Oh, it's not because of the scary costumes or pumpkin carving or the arrival of fall or anything like that. Halloween is the annual kick-off of the holiday candy season, which every parent knows lasts straight through winter and ends shortly after Easter.

Every year I plan to cut down on my family's windfall of candy by taking my children trick-or-treating to only five houses. Six tops. So it always comes as somewhat of a surprise when, two hours later, we find ourselves wandering up and down unfamiliar streets three towns over.

"Just one more house," they beg. "Please? I bet they have the really good candy there."

Then I watch as my children, who are usually scared of pin-head sized spiders and sleeping in the dark, charge straight through rubber witch heads, howling ghosts, and Styrofoam headstones for the sake of free candy.

Mind you, this is just the kind of at-all-costs attitude that always lands us at home with enough candy to keep everyone in a sugar coma until mid spring.

So this year, as an educated, conscientious parent, the first thing I did after sorting through the candy for potential hazards, was to stash it all in the freezer.

"Wha-at are you doing?" my daughter asked, horrified. "We can't eat frozen candy."

"Exactly."

You see, every parent knows that the most important thing about holiday candy left hanging around the house is that you need some kind of a system to dole it out. Left unguarded, my children wouldn't rest until every last piece was gone.

"You can eat a few pieces a day," I explained in my best take-charge tone. "But that's it."

They were outraged.

Of course, one of the big drawbacks to being a good role model is that you're expected to adhere to your own rules. It would be both unfair and hypocritical if I ate any of the Halloween candy while they were gone.

Which is exactly why I considered the Twix bar, which I ate the next day while they were at school, more of a reward.

The same goes for the Hershey's Kisses that I popped into my mouth after I folded the laundry—one for each sock.

For lunch I sampled two bags of chocolate covered raisins (more of a health food than candy, really). Then, after that, I washed down a miniature 3 Musketeers Bar with a pack of malt balls as a reward to myself for ironing.

Of course this would've all been fine except minutes before my children were due home from school I realized most of the A-list chocolate candy had somehow disappeared. And how, I ask you, could I explain that?

So, in desperation, I figured out a simple plan: I called my neighbor, Julie, who loves chewy candy.

"I'll give you seven boxes of Jujubes for a Snickers bar and a package of Reeses Peanut Butter Cups," I hissed into the phone. "Toss in a few Tootsie Rolls and it's a deal."

Then I called Ellen next door who likes gum, and traded a pack of jawbreakers for two bags of peanut M&M's.

Luckily, life being what it is, everyone's A-list candy is different. Which means that with a little tenacity, I'll be able to restock my children's candy supply before they get home.

Oh, sure, there's a message in here somewhere.

Maybe it's that parents shouldn't implement rules they can't follow. Or maybe it's that holidays should be celebrated in another, less tangible, way. Or maybe, just maybe, it's that parents should stick to eating only the candy that no one in the family will miss.

Whatever the reason I can't worry about it now. I only have five minutes to exchange seven packets of candy corn for three rolls of Lifesavers, then trade up for a half dozen Pixy Stix, which should just about equal the one Butterfinger bar I accidentally ate while walking down the driveway to the mailbox.

I just hope that Easter comes early this year.

Thanksgiving Traditions

I haven't wanted to bring this up, but something strange happens to people on Thanksgiving. I don't mean that they suddenly change their hair color and go on shopping sprees or anything like that, I mean that something compels otherwise reasonable people to make the same traditional family Thanksgiving stuffing recipe year after year, no matter what.

If you don't believe me, ask my friend Kathy. Most of the rest of the year she successfully tries to avoid cooking. But each Thanksgiving she wakes up at dawn and spends *hours* in the kitchen making Wild Rice Stuffing with Pearl Onions and Bacon Bits, a traditional family recipe that's been passed down from mother to daughter for five generations.

"Why don't you just sleep in and buy a container of instant stuffing mix?" I suggested one day over coffee.

But I could tell by the way she rolled her eyes and said, "But that's not the way we do it" that it would just be plain wrong.

Then there's Kathleen. For as long as I've known her she's had a policy of adding handfuls of olives to her stuffing. Oh, not because of any special flavor or because her family particularly likes them but because, "That's what my mother always did." It doesn't seem to matter that her mother actually hates olives and has no idea why she did it that way either.

But things could be worse. Due to a cruel twist of fate, my friend Carol's husband insisted on bringing along his own family's stuffing recipe when they got married. Since Carol didn't want to bother making two different batches, she decided to merge them together, and now her Thanksgiving stuffing is a mostly inedible concoction of Brazil nuts, buttermilk, chopped onions, and pineapple.

There are, of course, always the exceptions. My neighbor Sue refuses to make any stuffing at all because last Thanksgiving her family's traditional Apple Almond Sage Stuffing recipe fell under suspicion. It started when she found out that a certain cousin, Heidi, follows a traditional recipe for Apple Walnut

Sausage Stuffing that was given to her by a great-aunt who was known for her orange-walnut-fennel stuffing. I ask you, how do you get to the bottom of that?

However, we all know what's clearly going on here. Thanksgiving stuffing, in a subtle way, connects each generation as few other foods can. Sure, over the years the recipes may change a bit, and you might not be able to explain exactly why you're supposed to add a cup of crushed oysters to the breadcrumbs, but that's okay, everyone just goes along with it anyway.

Then, of course, there are people like me, whose traditional family stuffing recipe comes from the back of a crouton box. I'm not sure what this says about my family—except that I come from a long line of people who can't cook. Or perhaps they're just practical. Either way it's not much of a legacy.

And truth be told, I'm not sure what to do about it except to try to change the recipe. In fact, this year I think I'll add a dash of vermouth and some dried cherries and maybe even an oyster or two.

And if my kids complain about it I'll just calmly explain that it's okay if they don't like it. In fact, they don't even have to eat it. The most important thing is that we're creating a new family tradition to pass on together.

Then again, we could all just leave and go to a restaurant.

Christmas Cards

Face it: it's that time of year again. And I don't just mean to trim trees or hang lights or buy gifts. I mean it's time to get out the gold pen and the holiday stamps and send out your annual Christmas cards.

Make no mistake about it, choosing the right card takes a lot of thought. Are you the type who likes cuddly baby animals, or more of a religious theme? Do you prefer reindeer, Santa Claus or winter snow scenes? Or are you, like my friend Shirley, more of the Gingerbread Man type?

So this year I've decided to bypass the whole card-choosing issue and do what any typical, proud mother would do: find a picture of my family and turn it into a card.

I started by sorting through last year's batch of pictures for one where my entire family looked happy, relaxed and well-tanned, preferably taken somewhere in nature. Not too much to ask, right? But, shockingly enough, after going through several stacks, you guessed it, I didn't find one single picture that fit these criteria. So I went back through and tried to find a picture with three of us smiling and one of us with good hair. Then a picture with most of us clean and sort of grimacing. And then finally just any picture that had all four of us in it fully dressed at the same time. Still nothing, except for one taken in the mid 90's on the day we brought my son home from the hospital. But this would only shock and confuse people.

It was obvious from all this that we'd have to get a new picture taken just for the card. So we all got into our good velvet clothes and I called my neighbor Linda to come over with her camera.

"Quick, come take our picture," I hissed into the phone. "Before someone gets a runny nose or sneezes or picks up the cat or something."

Now Linda is an avid picture taker so you'd think that chances are, *one* picture would turn out decent enough to be used as a Christmas card. And you can imagine my surprise when I got the photographs back and saw 24 pictures of a rather surprised looking red-eyed family standing in front of various household appliances.

So I took matters into my own hands and moved on to plan number two: take pictures of the kids outside among all of the festive holiday decorations.

Mind you, I use the term "festive" loosely since all we had in front of our house was a string of colored light bulbs put up sometime in 1992.

Then I remembered the upscale neighborhood three blocks away where each year everyone went overboard with lawn decorations. It was a brilliant plan.

"You can't take pictures of our children in front of stranger's houses," my husband said. "What will our friends think?"

"That we got a bigger house and trendier Christmas lights?"

"Very funny."

The good news is that these pictures came out great. I had fabulous shots of my children posing in front of cutout wooden snowmen, reindeer, and even between the Three Wise Men in a miniature cardboard manger.

The bad news is that in the end, my husband was right. It just seemed, well, deceitful to send those out. Instead I chose a rather plain picture of the kids sitting on the living room floor holding an ornament.

But that's okay. You see, today I received a photo Christmas card from my old college friend Lisa who lives in a condo in South Florida. It was a lovely scene of her family gathered around a cozy fireplace mantel, holding a cat. Except that, as far as I know, she doesn't own a cat or, for that matter, a fireplace. In fact, now that I take a closer look, I'm not even sure that's her real husband.

And somehow that comforts me.

The Annual Picking of the Tree

It's that time of year again. And, no, I don't mean for shopping or putting up lights up or breaking out the good snow boots. Nooooooo. I mean it's time for an annual ritual so stressful and confusing that chances are, afterwards you will be found tucked under the ottoman humming and braiding your hair. I'm talking about the annual Picking of the Christmas Tree.

Now those of you who've done this without kids are probably thinking, "What's so bad about that? You just go to the lot, pick one, and voilà!"

Ha! Ha! I say.

Once you have kids, the Picking of the Tree is one of the most mind-boggling of experiences, parallel only to watching Madonna videos or counting presidential votes in Florida.

Let me explain.

Each year, not being organized or outdoorsy types, we usually wait until the last possible minute before choosing our tree from one of the lots in the middle of a discount store parking lot (which everyone knows is just like going to the forest, except for all of the shopping carts and halogen lights).

Oh sure, everything always starts out fine. We eagerly enter the lot filled with holiday spirit and high hopes. Heck, we may even make it past a tree or two in this very same mood. But, inevitably, someone will point and say something upsetting like, "Hey, what about this one?" and a major fight breaks out.

I'm not sure why this always surprises me because, let's face it, there is something about the Picking of the Tree that causes even the most blasé person to suddenly have a wildly passionate opinion.

Take, for instance, my ten-year-old daughter. Mind you, she's the type of person who doesn't even know that trees exist at any other time of the year. But, come December, she must find one that's exactly six feet tall, at least 24 inches in diameter, with bluish-green needles and preferably in the *Pinus strobus* family.

Then there's my seven-year-old son who claims he doesn't care what kind of tree we get as long as it doesn't look too tall, too short, too bushy, too twiggy, too green, too flocked or too much like, well, a tree.

But don't feel sorry for me. Save it for my friend Julie. After spending three hours meticulously studying every tree (including the ones planted between the cars in the parking lot), breaking up six fist fights and getting two dozen splinters in her hands, her kids suddenly decided that the only true, ecologically correct thing to do would be to go to the local nursery and buy a live tree.

Maybe I should be more like my friend Barb. At her house when she says, "Why don't we go get the tree?" her husband sighs, then goes into the garage and pulls down a cardboard box. Then the whole family spends a nice, non-stressful evening drinking hot apple cider and unfolding branches.

But where, I ask you, is the adventure in that?

Face it, despite the cold and all of the yelling, there's something special about picking out a Christmas tree together. I'm not sure why. Maybe it's from the anticipation. Or perhaps it's from being outside in the fresh air. Or maybe it's the effect of the fumes from all the cans of flocking.

Whatever the reason one thing's for certain: once the tree is decorated, no one cares what kind it is anymore. In fact, by the time New Year's Eve rolls around, people go out of their way to avoid it altogether.

Nobody ever said that the Picking of the Tree was supposed to make sense.

The Mystery of Easter Grass

Easter's on the way, and you know what that means: hard-boiled eggs, chocolate bunnies and *Easter grass*, lots and lots of Easter grass. And by that I don't mean the kind that comes from wheat seeds that you grow in a container on your kitchen sink. Noooooo. I mean the cellophane type that comes in a bag that you get in the holiday section of the grocery store. Of course, no one sets out to buy a ton of plastic Easter grass. Me, I usually buy a bag or two—just enough to fill my children's baskets. But let me warn you about Easter grass. As soon as you let it out of the bag and into the fresh air, it expands! And what you thought just a moment ago was the right amount to fill up one, maybe two baskets can now easily cover most of the state of Rhode Island.

If you think I'm exaggerating, just ask my friend Shirley. She naïvely left an open bag of "Floppy's Purple Easter Grass" on her kitchen table and went to change the laundry. When she came back only five minutes later, it had worked its way into the family room, over the recliner, and was heading down the hallway after the cat. "I'm not sure, but I think it wanted to take over the children's room," she said to me one day over coffee. "But I managed to corral it in the linen closet with a broom."

And don't think for one minute that you can solve anything by stuffing all the loose grass back into its original bag and putting on a twist tie. Any fool knows that no matter how hard you push and squeeze and beg, it won't fit back in the bag.

Sure, you can always try to throw it away immediately after Easter, but this, my friends, usually won't work either. In fact, last year I dumped all of our leftover Easter grass in the garbage can, jammed on the lid and immediately wheeled it to the curb. Days later I found suspicious purple strands sticking out of the washing machine and lying on top of the television set and waiting next to the shower and tucked underneath the organic lettuce in the crisper. I ask you, how do you explain that? It's astonishing that we live in a society that can clone sheep and send a man to the moon, but we can't figure out how to control *Easter grass.*

Naturally, you could always bypass the whole issue by growing real Easter grass from rye seed, but that would just bring up a whole new set of problems—the kind that make worrying about a little extra plastic grass in your home seem, well, silly.

Besides, there are lots of practical uses for it like, say, packing material or hair on paper bag puppets. Some people even stuff the toes of their good pumps with it or in some cases, use it as extra insulation in the attic. Once, my friend Julie even used it to make pom-poms for her daughter who wanted to be a cheerleader for Halloween. The other nice thing about plastic Easter grass is that just when you've grown tired and weary of picking it up, it mysteriously disappears. But don't get your hopes up. It would be a stretch to say it was gone for good. In fact, my theory is that it doesn't really go away at all. It merely hibernates in the walls for a few months until it's time to reappear disguised as Christmas tinsel.

Trust me, crazier things have happened.

SUMMERTIME AND THE LIVIN' AIN'T SO EASY

Unsuitable

The end of spring marks the beginning of the most dreaded time of the year: bathing suit season. Shopping for a new suit is the most humiliating experience since getting on the doctor's scale in the ninth month of pregnancy. Last year's suit always seems to shrink a few sizes during the long winter months, but I put off the inevitable until the heat makes it impossible for me to keep wearing leggings and a long sweatshirt to the beach.

On the first hundred-degree day, I reluctantly enter a department store with my children and try to inconspicuously look for the section containing the Lycra instruments of torture.

"May I help you?" asks a teenage salesperson, who is the width of a twig.

"Not unless you're Mother Nature."

"Oh, I see," she nods sympathetically. "The bathing suits are over there." She points to a display of spandex that looks similar to a bunch of multi-colored rubber bands.

"Thank you, " I mumble and walk towards the rack.

"One or two piece?" the salesgirl continues, following closely behind.

"Four." I hold a suit, marked with my size, against me. "Either this is mis-marked or someone was kidding," I pause, "I need a swimsuit that says 'washing machine' not 'sex machine.'"

I watch the salesgirl leaf quickly through the racks.

"I need something that's a cross between Wonder Bra, corset and camouflage," I continue.

"Speedo or OP?" she asks. "Bikini or French cut?"

"How about, 'The Mother of Two?'" I pause. "Something the color of spit up, with an elastic tummy, detachable long skirt (that doubles as a canopy or burp cloth), water-proof pockets for snacks and diapers, sippy cup holders on either hip, and 'No Whining' printed in red letters across the front."

"Well," she stammers, "How about these?" She hands me a brightly colored one-piece that looks similar to the Brazilian flag, a suit made out of Barnum and Bailey's circus tent, and a bikini that would strangle a Chihuahua. She guided me to the dressing room where I grunted, groaned, pushed and tucked my way into the suits. One hour and two hernias later I found a suit that fit, let me breathe, and would've looked great—without my body in it.

As I looked in the full-length mirror at my post-partum tummy and legs that had more stretch marks than the San Andreas Fault, I saw my children sitting on the bench in the dressing room making funny faces in the mirror.

"You look like Barbie," my daughter said, watching me.

"Barbie," echoed my son.

I smiled and realized that my children didn't see my faults. My blemishes weren't deformities, they were birthmarks, and my varicose veins were Purple Hearts in the battle of reproduction.

"I'll take it!" I cried from inside the dressing room. I didn't look younger or thinner. I looked like what I was: the mother of two. And it suited me just fine.

_A_ Housewife's Mid Summer Prayer

Prayer of a Stay-at-Home Mother in Mid August

Dear God, grant me the strength to last until Back-to-School Night.

Give me the energy to drive the swim team carpool, take knots out of wet shoelaces with my teeth, and untangle the dog from the sprinkler hose.

Grant me the wisdom to remember the name of the kid from down the street who hasn't left our house since July.

Walk with me through the backyard over piles of wet bathing suits and empty ice cream cups, to rescue my good lipstick from the bottom of the wading pool.

Give me the courage to accept that everything in the refrigerator either has a bite out of it, a finger stuck in it, or is reproducing in the vegetable crisper underneath the expensive cheese.

Guide me down the hallway to the laundry room, where I can experience five minutes of peace and quiet by turning the lights out and climbing on the dryer so the kids can't see my feet underneath the door.

Help me accept the fact that even if I take the kids to the circus, install a pool in the backyard, go on a safari, and carve a redwood tree into a canoe and sail down the Congo—my children will end each day with, "I'm bored."

Grant me the serenity to smile when my husband insists on tossing the hamburger helper on the gas grill because, "everything tastes better barbecued."

Give me the fortitude to sit through eighty-five hours of swim lessons and watch as my children backstroke around the pool the same amount of miles it would take to reach Communist China.

Smile down on me the day my husband decides to take the family camping in the wilderness for three days with nothing but a tent, a few sleeping bags, and a cooler full of potato chips and Pepsi.

And when it rains (and You know it will, God) lead me to the nearest 7-Eleven to buy the umbrellas my husband refused to pack because "only an idiot" would expect a storm in the middle of the summer during a drought year.

In Your infinite wisdom, show me how to disconnect the video game console that hasn't been turned off since June twenty-second.

Grant me the patience to not rip the car stereo out of the dashboard with my teeth when my husband listens to "Louie, Louie" for the hundred and eighty-sixth time, cranked up at full volume.

Comfort me when I realize that the color of my earth tone carpet has changed into a mixture of melted blue Popsicle and the remains of somebody's purple slush.

And if I ask too much God, just give me the foresight to know that one day the barbecue, the television, and the sprinkler hose will be off; the refrigerator, the front door, and the garage will be closed, and I'll wonder where my children (and the little red-headed boy with the glasses) went.

The Tankini

I've been lying on a lounge chair at the neighborhood pool for three hours and fifteen minutes—and I'm not getting up.

Call me wild and crazy, but this summer I gave in and purchased the latest fashion phenomenon: the tankini, a two-piece bathing suit with the "tank" being the top and the "ini" being the bottom.

This really shocked my family since I'm never in fashion—and the last time I wore a two-piece bathing suit it had cute little fishies on it, and I was propped up in a plastic wading pool sucking my thumb.

I never follow trends and I still can't figure out what possessed me to follow this one. Maybe it was the thrill of finally taking off a few pounds during the long winter months. Maybe it was the excitement of the start of a new summer. Maybe it was a desperate attempt to stave off middle age. But I have a hunch it was one of those impulse purchases people are always warning me about.

My friend Julie once went into a discount store for one pack of film and came out with a light-up moon globe, a food dehydrator, a John Tesh CD, and a Chia Pet.

I never understood how this could happen to someone as sane and intelligent as Julie until the day I was strolling through a department store aisle and saw a rack of two piece bathing suits, with pictures of Kathy Ireland fastened onto the tags and a big sign that said "30% OFF." I could've walked around it, but the thought immediately flashed through my mind that if I bought a tankini—right now—I could save money and have the same bathing suit as a supermodel. Plus all of my problems would be solved: the house would stay clean, the laundry would be finished, and I would probably have better thighs. In the heat of the moment I grabbed a suit off the rack and brought it to the cashier. This was my first big mistake.

My second one was showing it to my children when I got home.

"What's that?" my daughter asked. "Some kind of sling shot?"

"Very funny," I said. "It's the latest thing in swimsuit fashion."

Then I went to my room, tried it on, and walked into the living room to show my family.

"What do you think?" I asked.

I bet they would've told me if they could have stopped laughing long enough to speak.

Eventually, my four-year-old son caught his breath and managed to blurt out, "I see your belly button!" before he fell over laughing again. But how can you trust the fashion judgment of someone who can't put on his own underpants?

I looked in the mirror and decided it didn't look too bad. Besides, this season might be the last chance I had to wear a two-piece suit before middle age crept in.

So, on the first day of summer, I wore it to the neighborhood pool.

It was great. I felt young, slim, and sexy. Then I took off my robe.

I quickly dove into the lounge chair and covered myself up with the towel.

"What are you doing, Honey?" my husband asked.

"What does it look like? I'm showing off my new suit," I said.

As I watched my family go into the pool, I tried to convince myself that if I lay really still and kept my eyes focused on my book, no one would see me.

But how do you explain to a four-year-old that you can't go into the pool with him because if you so much as move an inch, everyone would notice your flabby, white stomach and know that it hasn't seen the light of day since the summer of '68, and you are definitely not qualified to wear a tankini.

So, I've been lying on a lounge chair for three hours and fifteen minutes and I'm not getting up—but I'm working on it.

Labor Day

Labor Day is really a holiday in disguise. At best, it's somewhat of a nebulous holiday. For example, some people (usually politicians and academic types) know it is a day to recognize and honor the American Labor Movement, while other people think of it as an extra day off work with pay. Still others (and you know who you are) have absolutely no idea what they're supposed to be celebrating, but think it might have something to do with a groundhog coming out of a hole to look for its shadow.

But let's face it, to mothers of school aged children Labor Day means only one thing: the end of summer vacation.

Frankly, by the beginning of September I'm tired of spending my days with a group of people who drip blue slushy on the good sofa and argue over who is breathing more air.

Labor Day is my cue to drain the wading pool and rescue my good lipstick from the bottom of the sandbox for the very last time. It serves as a wakeup call to get the children back on a regular schedule and off to bed at a decent hour in this time zone.

Another thing about Labor Day is that, unlike any other time of the year, I'm at the peak of my game. My children haven't been late for school yet or missed any homework assignments. And I'm still considered a reliable member of the carpool.

Plus I no longer have to care about what I look like in a bathing suit. I can go back to my old pre-summer ways of wearing long pants with elastic waistbands over my pasty white legs. The world will no longer see that my stomach is pale and flabby and that the backs of my thighs have the same texture as Play-Doh that's been run over by a waffle iron.

Let me tell you, Labor Day isn't just a holiday; it's a declaration of freedom.

If you don't believe me just ask my friend Julie, a loving, doting mother, who celebrates Labor Day by singing "Hallelujah!" and shoving her three children into the backseat of the car and speeding off to the nearest store for school supplies.

And it's not just Julie. My friend Linda catapults out of bed on Labor Day morning and immediately begins sifting her children's sandbox for all of her good silverware.

Of course people without children can't really understand this. They don't see how we can celebrate the end of long, lazy days of nice weather, swimming, and trips to the beach.

But I have a feeling it's because they didn't spend the last three months playing cruise director for a group of energetic tourists with the attention span of, say, four seconds.

However, on top of marking the end of summer vacation, Labor Day also causes me to slow down and savor the summer days that are left. There is something about it that adds a certain *joie de vivre* to barbecues and swim meets that just wasn't there in mid June.

I'm not sure why this is. Maybe it's human nature to want things you can't have. Or perhaps the end of summer makes people more introspective. Or maybe it's because I know relief is in sight.

No matter what the reason, there will always be some people who treat Labor Day as an opportunity to honor the American Labor Movement and others who consider it just another excuse to stay home from work.

But, between you and me, if you ever want to know the true meaning of the holiday, just ask a mother of a school-aged child.

The Theme Park Vacation

Face it, something strange happens when you take your family on vacation to a theme park. Oh, I'm not talking about Big Foot sightings or alien abductions or anything like that. I'm talking about the strange thing that happens to otherwise reasonable people who are suddenly willing pay exorbitant prices to experience the very same conditions they strive to avoid the rest of the year. It's bizarre, I tell you.

I mean, when else would you ever purposely wait at the end of a line that wraps all the way around the outside of a grocery store and ends somewhere past the shopping cart corral in the parking lot, only to hand someone at the register an obscene amount of money? If you're like most people, your answer is probably the uncensored version of, "Not on your life, Lady!" And I don't blame you. During any other time in my life, if there are more than three people waiting in front of me, my left eye begins to twitch and what little time I have left on this planet begins to flash forward before my eyes.

But for some reason lines are okay as long as I'm on "vacation."

And that's not all. Visiting a theme park makes me do other bizarre things. Like actually seeking out something that will fling me from side to side until I'm nauseous, then spray me with water. Call me crazy, but I usually go to great lengths to avoid this happening to me. In fact, I try my utmost to always remain dry and upright.

So why then do I travel hundreds of miles, spend one sixth of my yearly income, and stand in line for hours to have this done to me when I could go into the backyard with my children, turn on the hose, and feel the same sensations for *free*?

Because, you guessed it, I'm on vacation!

On top of that, all year long I never ever walk anywhere. Every time I try to walk down the street to the park I last two, maybe three blocks, before I break out in a sweat, my knees begin to wobble, and I end up turning back to get my car and a nice cup of cappuccino.

But mind you, at a theme park something mysterious happens. I suddenly metamorphose into a Decathlon runner, sprinting across acres and acres of parking lots to get to the entrance gate with a ten-pound backpack strapped to me, just so I can beat the crowd of people waiting for the tram. And I don't even need to remind you about the countless laps from wherever we are to the "good" ride somewhere across the park.

And it doesn't stop there. I've watched my husband, a frugal man who clips coupons and stocks up on cans of tuna fish, voluntarily pay a bazillion dollars for a stick of cotton candy and a corn dog.

And my friend Julie, a person so afraid of heights she refuses to take elevators in buildings with more than two floors, actively seeks out a ride that will shoot her body fifty feet into the air and then plummet two-thirds of it to the ground, leaving most of her lungs and spinal column dangling in midair.

No one knows why this happens. I mean, if it's thrills you seek, the car ride there should fulfill you enough. You would think that no ride, however horrendous, could top being trapped for hours in an enclosed space with two bored, tiny people in the backseat who are kicking your seat, flinging crayon shards into your hair, and having sporadic fits of screaming.

The one sure thing about visiting theme parks is that for some unexplainable reason, next year you'll do it all again. The lines, the crowds, the food—everything.

Oh, it's not because you're stupid or a fool, even though you might feel that way. It's because deep down, being hurled through the air in a plastic bucket the shape of a rocket really *is* fun. Plus, it builds precious family memories for your children.

And, sometimes, that's the price you have to pay.

Lost Summer Stuff

It never fails. Fall is the time of year when people stop whatever it is they're doing and take stock of their surroundings. Not because they're particularly neat or organized mind you, but because that's when they suddenly realize that most of the things in their houses don't belong to them.

Let me explain. At my house, summer passes in a flurry of barbecues, pool parties, and other back yard events. And naturally, people leave things behind: a beach towel here, a pair of sunglasses there. But then one day, usually in the fall, I suddenly take a good long look around and realize that my house is filled with all sorts of things I don't remember owning. It's filled with mystery snorkel gear and swim fins and sandals and faded tee shirts and all that. In other words: Lost Summer Stuff. And it's not like you can just give these things back, mind you. Everyone knows that the major rule about Lost Summer Stuff is that no one, *no one* ever claims it.

And, really, that wouldn't be so bad except, let's face it, no one ever loses anything really useful. I've yet to search my house after a party and come across, say, a Prada handbag floating in the pool. Usually the stuff I find is of the plastic inflatable toy variety.

Oh all right, I take that back. Once during a certain potluck barbecue, my friend Shirley left a pair of high-end sterling salad tongs sitting on the chaise lounge. But that doesn't really count because eventually she remembered where she had left them and insisted on taking them back.

But again I digress.

Naturally, the major problem with harboring Lost Summer Stuff is figuring out what to do with it all. Oh sure, you could try calling every person who's been to your house in the last five months or so and ask them if they're missing a bikini: polka dots with pink ruffled panties, size three. Go ahead. Try it.

Or you could be like my friend Monica, a slightly superstitious sort of person with lots of extra storage space, who has four boxes filled with unclaimed snorkels, broken sandals, and swim goggles. She refuses to throw anything away because she's convinced the very second the garbage truck rounds the corner, the owner will suddenly remember leaving it at her house and ask for it back. And how would she explain that?

Then again you could listen to my friend Sue, whose solution for lost summer stuff is to use it.

"It never fails," she said." "As soon as you use something that's not yours, the rightful owner will magically appear and exclaim to everyone around you, 'Oh there's my favorite plastic Hawaiian punch bowl! I've been looking for that for ages.'"

Then they gloat in the same "I caught you" sort of way that FBI agents do when questioning members of organized crime.

If you ask me, the best way to get rid of *Lost Summer Stuff* is to discreetly bring it to other friends' and neighbors' houses and leave it there. Chances are, it'll eventually work its way back to the right place.

In fact, just the other day I managed to conveniently leave a pair of mismatched plastic tumblers at my neighbor's housewarming party, and a pair of tennis shoes at my friend Carol's potluck.

But let me just say, that doesn't mean that I'm completely off the hook. For instance, this morning I found a familiar looking slightly-faded Budweiser towel peeking out from underneath the potted geraniums that I swear I had inconspicuously left in someone else's backyard last summer.

But I'm not too worried. I'll just put it in the trunk along with the inflatable water wings and the Scooby Doo socks.

Thank goodness the holiday party season is coming up.

SCHOOL DAYS, SCHOOL DAYS, DEAR OLD GOLDEN RULE DAYS...

Mom's First Day of School

"The Kindergarten registration packets are here," I announced over the phone to my friend, "and they're going faster than tickets to a Rolling Stones concert!"

I slammed the phone down, buckled my daughter into the car, and drove to the neighborhood elementary school where I pulled in behind three campers, two RV trailers, and a tent.

"How long have you been here?" I asked the mother at the head of the line.

"Since 3:00 a.m.," she answered. "I've been waiting for this day since my twin boys threw the cat down the laundry chute with my panty hose and set the backyard on fire with a magnifying glass, lighter fluid, and my silk negligee."

I nodded in understanding. I often dreamed of having time to write a best-selling novel, learn to paint like Picasso, or wear earrings and brush my teeth in the same day.

"Mommy!" my daughter urgently grasped my hand. "I don't want to go to school! I won't like it!" She stamped her foot.

"You'll love it!" I assured her, "You'll have a great time and make a lot of new friends."

A few hours later we reached the front of the line, and received a packet and a pen. I bent over the counter and filled in the information as my daughter impatiently tugged at my dress.

"Please!" she cried. "Don't make me go!"

I quickly filled in the blanks and gave the secretary the completed forms.

"School begins next Monday at 8:00 o'clock," she said, smiling. "Kindergarten is in room one."

I nodded and took my daughter's hand.

"Don't make me go," she begged all the way to the car as I began to plan my hours of freedom going shopping, having manicures, and taking classes. I would do it all!

I spent the rest of the week taking my daughter for daily walks to the school playground, reading every book I could find about Kindergarten, and trying to convince my daughter that learning the alphabet, counting to one hundred, and getting to paint with your fingers was more fun than staying home with me.

On Monday morning my daughter stood by the front door in a new dress, patent leather shoes, and tears.

"It's time to go!" I gently took her hand and guided her out the door to the car.

"Mommy, can I have a drink of water?" she begged.

"No," I said buckling her into the back seat. "I'm not falling for that!"

"Can we go to the park instead?"

I firmly shook my head.

When we approached her new classroom, she clung to my legs like Velcro.

"Mommy," she whispered, "please stay with me."

"I can't, honey. But look!" I nudged her forward and pointed into the room.

"There's your friend, Stephanie, waving to you!"

My daughter looked up through her tears and began to smile.

"There's Ryan, too!" I pushed her gently inside.

My daughter wiped her tears on her sleeve as she began to enter the room and walk toward her friends.

"Bye, Mom," she called without looking back.

I stood in the doorway and watched her sit down on the carpet with the other children.

Wait! I thought frantically. *Don't go!*

She smiled and blew a kiss.

Are you still thirsty? I'll bring you a drink of water.

The children looked at their teacher and began to sing and clap their hands.

I have time for a story or a walk to the park.

She waved happily between claps.

Stay with me . . . a little longer.

The singing stopped and my daughter smiled at the teacher.

"Good-bye! Have a great day!" I called from the doorway as I turned to leave. Then I carefully wiped the tears off my cheek with the small, pink sweater I still clutched in my hands.

⊛ff Color

The week my daughter started kindergarten, I should have been suspicious when the teacher sent home a note that said:

Dear Parents,

I know how anxious you are to take part in your child's education. For the next two weeks we will be studying colors. Each day your child will receive a colored piece of paper and a short homework assignment. Please help them complete it and send your child to school dressed in the color the following day.

I wanted to be an active and involved parent, so when my daughter came home with a square of yellow paper I went to the store and bought her a cute yellow dress with a matching bow and socks. Then I told her everything I knew about yellow.

"It is a primary color," I said. "It also means yield. It's the color of the sun and ducks, and it once was the color of the squash and bananas in the crisper."

"Cool." She drew the pictures on the worksheet.

Blue Day followed. We spent an hour looking around the house for something blue, but all we could find was a batch of penicillin growing on the cheese in the refrigerator. She finally drew a picture of the sky and I sent her to school dressed in denim.

The next day we were late for school because my daughter wanted to wear her ballet leotard and feather boa instead of the cute red dress I bought. After negotiating for over an hour, I finally talked her down to a T-shirt with a cool catsup stain. As soon as she was dressed, I realized we hadn't drawn any red objects on her homework paper so I scribbled on it with my lipstick as I ran to the car.

By Thursday, I learned my lesson and dressed her in green leggings and a sweater while she was still asleep. She completed the homework sheet in the car on the way to school by digging around on the floorboard for an old piece of gum to tape to the paper. I started to wonder if my efforts were really enhancing her education.

Each color became more difficult.

"That's not white," she said pointing to a shirt I pulled from her drawer. "It's light gray."

"It's 'Farmer White,'" I said, "made from a mixture of pure white, black, brown, and navy blue cotton fabric thrown in hot water and laundry detergent. It was invented by your father."

On Purple Day she insisted on going to school in my old negligee tucked into sweat pants, and a pair of patent leather shoes. The only accessory missing was an empty beer bottle in a brown paper bag. I began to hate public education.

By Orange Day my daughter was out of secondary-color clothes, so I pulled a pink shirt out of her closet and handed it to her.

"This is orange," I lied.

When my daughter finally came home from school and announced she was finished studying colors, I felt like throwing my arms out to my sides and bursting into song, like Julie Andrews in *The Sound of Music*.

"The teacher said we could wear our favorite color tomorrow for the Rainbow Party," my daughter said. "Why are you dancing like that, Mommy?"

"No reason. Which color would you like to wear?" (Anything had to be easier than orange.)

She twisted her hair around her fingers and thought for a moment.

"Cerulean," she said.

I couldn't wait for summer vacation.

Sharing Day

Okay, so it's time for your child's first week of kindergarten. You already bought the new backpack, lunch pail and pencil case. And, like any good parent, you also bought packs of new pencils, erasers, ink pens, colored markers, binders and metallic star stickers. In brief, you've done everything to prepare your child for his or her academic career.

But wait! Not so fast. There's just one more teeny tiny detail you need to know about school that isn't on any of the lists they give you. You will need objects—lots and lots of objects. Why? Because it's kindergarten and chances are, there'll be sharing there. Lots and lots of sharing. And not just casual sharing, mind you. More than likely your child will be encouraged to share every day, five days a week, for the thirty-something weeks that make up the school year. Which, calculated out, means that approximately 5,387 bazillion objects will be hauled from your house to the kindergarten class where they will endure the scrutiny of *other people*.

Let me just warn you: lesser parents have cracked under the pressure.

Sure, at first it's easy to find things lying around the house that are politically correct and socially acceptable: A postcard from your last vacation. A pair of binoculars. A fun hat. A few foreign coins. Maybe if you get real lucky, a bird nest or something else from nature.

Really, it seems as if you could go on like this forever. But then it happens: you run out of "good stuff." The first sign is when your child brings a petrified cheese stick from the deli drawer. Next it's an old Elvis eight track. Then before you know it, you're sending your child off to school with a bottle of catsup dressed in a Barbie ball gown.

The way I see it, when this happens you have three choices. Your first choice is to tell your child in your best I'm-in-charge voice to skip sharing. That it's much more fun to listen than to share anyway.

"Ha, ha," the child will say. Any five-year-old knows that Show and Tell gives structure and meaning to kindergarten life and any kid without something to share risks losing his place on the rug, or in line or, worse yet, being ignored altogether.

The second option is to recycle the stuff you already sent, this time thinly disguised. This isn't as tricky as you might think. Most kindergartners won't recognize the plastic camel your child brought to share way back in September—especially now that it's wearing lipstick. But the problem with this is that you're bound to be found out. One day a kid will see right through the gold lamé and masking tape and say, "Hey, didn't I see that stuffed poodle before?" Then your child will be humiliated since he or she broke the number-one-rule-of-sharing: things can only be brought once.

Then of course, you can always do what I do: work a trade with an equally desperate parent who has a child in another class.

In fact, just the other morning I got what some would call a peculiar phone call.

"Hello?" I said.

"I have a picture of a beached whale and a bag of sea shells," my friend Susie hissed on the other end of the receiver. "What do you have?"

"A homemade bird feeder and a rock from the Grand Canyon."

"Deal," she said, and hung up.

Oh, all right, maybe it's a little sneaky. Some people may even say it's just plain wrong—especially those of you who have closets full of vacation souvenirs. But me, I prefer to think of it more as "pooling available resources."

And, hey, if that's not the true spirit of sharing, I don't know what is.

Share and Share Alike

I've told you before about sharing, but I *have* to tell you about my son.

When my son started preschool, he was introduced to several new activities that the teacher assured me were essential for fostering high self-esteem and a sound academic development. I had no problem with this, but I started to worry when the teacher informed me that my son had to choose an object from home to share with the class once a week.

The day before my son's first sharing experience, I wandered through the house looking for something he could take that would show we were an interactive, functional family that did more on weekends than sit on the sofa in our pajamas watching the Cartoon Network. After two hours I couldn't find anything appropriate, so I went to the craft store and bought the most politically correct, socially acceptable item I could find: a birdhouse kit.

We started putting it together that afternoon, but my son fell asleep before it was finished and I spent the rest of the evening frantically nailing it together.

The next morning my son came downstairs, rubbed the sleep from his eyes and stared at it. "What's that?" he asked.

"It's your sharing," I said. "When it's your turn, just say you built this with Mommy to feed the wild birds in our well-maintained backyard and you've developed a deep appreciation for nature, okay?"

My son nodded as I stuffed it into his backpack.

Everything was going great until the teacher called my son into the middle of the circle to take his turn. He wrapped his arms around the backpack and refused to move. The only thing that came out of his mouth was a tiny whimper.

I thought my son might be less shy if he chose what he brought next time. So the following week I sent him to his room to find something he'd like to share. He returned brandishing his Bazooka squirt gun.

I pictured the other children standing in the middle of the circle sharing handmade family projects, educational toys or cute stuffed animals with names like Fluffy or Snuggles, while my son swaggered around looking like the Terminator.

"How about something from the backyard?" I quickly led him outside.

After searching through the tanbark, he finally found an interesting stick. I convinced him to put it into his backpack before he changed his mind.

The next day, when it was his turn, he slowly opened his backpack and took out the stick.

"How interesting," the teacher said. "Can you tell us about it?"

He nodded. Then he slowly lifted it up and pretended to pull the trigger. "Bang!" he cried. I decided next time I would give him a little more guidance.

The following week I scoured the house for something intriguing that couldn't be turned into a weapon. I finally managed to coerce him into sharing a picture of Yosemite I had taken during our last vacation.

I figured my son couldn't shoot anything with it and everyone could see we were an outdoorsy, peaceful family who enjoyed nature without the use of firearms.

This time a little boy with a soccer trophy went first. "My team won first place," he said sweetly.

Then a girl passed around a terrarium made out of recycled two liter bottles. "My Mommy helped me make this so I could learn about the water cycle."

I couldn't wait for my son's turn. Soon everyone would know we were a normal, nature-loving, college-bound family. I held my breath as he pulled the picture out of his backpack.

"Can you tell us where that is?" the teacher asked.

He held it up and shook his head as if he'd never seen it before. Then his eyes lit up with a spark of recognition.

"It was cool! That's where my dad locked the keys in the car." He excitedly pointed to the picture. "And my mom got real mad and said lots of bad words." He grinned widely.

I had a feeling this was going to be a long year.

Major Project

I took an active role in my daughter's education when she started kindergarten. I handled bake sales, field trips, and classroom snacks like a pro. Everything was going great until the day my daughter brought home her first family art project.

My family, whose members take five days to put a glass in the dishwasher, had less than 24 hours to decorate a scarecrow. I nervously read the directions on the homework note.

Step one: "Cut and paste arms and legs onto body." I wasn't fooled. All family projects start out easy to lure the parent into a false sense of security.

Step two: "Color neatly in the lines." I became more suspicious.

Step three: "Decorate the scarecrow using items found around the house." I braced myself.

Step four: "Work as a family and use your imagination. The projects will be displayed in the cafeteria during the school Harvest Festival." Rats, I knew it.

Translated into parent-talk, it meant the whole school would know my family is artistically impaired with the fine motor skills and creative ability of a pack of Rhesus monkeys. It also meant my family's project would probably be displayed alongside a scarecrow with two interchangeable matching outfits and custom shoes created by a family distantly related to Martha Stewart.

I sneered at the smiling mimeographed scarecrow in his jaunty straw hat, and called an emergency family meeting to gather our forces.

"Let's split up and see what we can find around the house to decorate the scarecrow," I said. "Meet back here when you've found something that doesn't move, bite, or smell."

Half an hour later, my daughter emerged from her room with a pair of purple Barbie shoes, my son brought in a handful of dry cat food from the back porch, my husband donated a fly-fishing lure, and I found two life savers and a wad of chewing gun in the family room sofa. We placed our supplies on the table along with a pair of pinking shears (I threw safety scissors away the day my son gave the cat bangs) and wallpaper seam glue (I used the last bottle of Elmer's to reattach three buttons to a sweater and shorten a pair of pants.)

We divided up the jobs: my daughter cut out the scarecrow's parts, my son arranged the pieces, my husband glued, and I tried to keep the cat from eating our supplies.

When we were done, our scarecrow was a work of art: a Picasso. Its legs were attached to its elbows and an arm stuck out of its ear. It had two lifesaver eyes, a chewing gum nose, cat food hair, a fishing lure mustache, and a pair of purple Barbie shoes for feet.

"It's perfect," my daughter said. "I can't wait to bring it to school."

I cringed, knowing I'd be instantly disqualified for mother of the year.

The next morning I waited with my daughter outside the classroom and listened to the other children discuss their projects. I stuffed ours into her backpack when I saw a girl heading our way, carrying a scarecrow with gold ribbon hair, felt patches on his hat, and a papier-mâché crow perched on his shoulder.

"My mother worked all night to finish this," the girl said. "Where's yours?"

My daughter pulled our scarecrow out. The girl silently considered it.

"What's that?" she said pointing to its head.

"Cat food."

The girl reached out and touched it.

"Cool."

I knew we'd passed the assignment with flying colors.

Friendship Fruit Salad

I couldn't wait to be a part of my son's preschool education and I'd looked forward to volunteering in his classroom since the beginning of the year. When it was finally my turn to help I wondered what exciting, educational task the teacher would assign me to do.

"You can facilitate making the friendship fruit salad," the teacher said when we arrived. "Just supervise the children when they cut the fruit into tiny pieces." She pointed to a table piled high with the various fruits the children had brought. "Then mix it together and serve it in paper cups for the snack at eleven o'clock."

The thought of being surrounded by a group of preschoolers with sharp objects made me nervous, but I smiled and nodded as the teacher explained that the children could wander among the different stations and choose their own activity at their own pace. When she was finished I divided the fruit into sections on cutting boards, rolled up my sleeves and waited for a group of preschoolers to wander my way.

Soon, two girls sat down at my table and I guided them to the sink to wash their hands. I turned on the water and scrubbed. They had a great time splashing and making bubbles with the soap. It took me fifteen minutes to rinse their hands, mop up the water on the floor (which turned into a tiny lake) and coerce them to go back to the fruit.

"This is a strawberry," I said as I demonstrated how to make tiny cuts. "It is a fruit and grows on bushes. Would you like to try?" I slid the cutting board in front of them.

One of the girls considered it for a moment, then reached over and popped it into her mouth. The other girl wandered away from the table to pet the rabbit.

I finished slicing the strawberries as a group of boys approached the table. *Finally*, I thought, *a golden opportunity to make a difference, to break down domestic stereotypes, and mold male thinking at a young age.*

"Cool." The boys said as they sat down. "Real knives."

I led them to the sink and handed them a wet paper towel that they squeezed to make a pattern on the floor with the water. After

I wiped it up, I led them back to the table and demonstrated how to chop bananas into tiny slices. This worked great until one of them figured out how to smash a piece on the top of his thumb and fling it at the boy across the table. As banana pieces went flying, I began to think of another name for Friendship Salad.

When I finished chopping the rest of the bananas I realized I only had twenty minutes to have the snack prepared and I still had a lot more fruit to slice.

I cruised around the room and tried to lure volunteers to my table to help.

"Would you like to work together to help prepare our snack?" I asked a group of children gathered around the water fountain.

No one moved.

"I'll let you have some grapes."

Silence.

"How about a peach?" My voice rose. "A cookie! A pair of roller-skates! A new bike!"

Finally three little girls slowly moved towards me. I spit on a tissue and quickly wiped their hands. Then I gave the girls an apple, cut it in half, and showed them how to find a star in the middle. Then I demonstrated how to cut it into tiny pieces. As they were cutting, a few more children wandered over and I showed them the star and gave them an apple.

I kept slicing until there was enough fruit to fill 25 cups. Then I quickly spooned it out and carried it outside to the children who were waiting on the grass.

"This is the result of your hard work and cooperation," I said.

Suddenly I was interrupted by a scream coming from one of the blankets.

"The banana is touching the apple!"

"I don't like grapes! Somebody get them out!"

"My orange has a bug on it!"

"That's a raisin."

"Gross!"

It was apparent that this salad was misnamed. As the children continued yelling I began to quickly gather the cups, and I hoped the next time I came to help, the teacher would give me an easier task—like explaining Einstein's theory of relativity.

Book Fair

I'm not quite sure how this happened, but somehow the PTA got a hold of my phone number.

Now don't get me wrong, they seem like a nice, friendly group of people, despite all those bake sales and cookie dough fundraisers. But apparently, since I work from home, they must figure that I have oodles of free time after I finish vacuuming and instead of aimlessly wandering around looking for activities to fill the empty void, my day could be much better spent, say, volunteering at the annual book fair.

And between you and me, they're probably right. But that's not why I let them talk me into doing it. Oh nooo. It was mainly because, (a) it would be a great way to get involved at my children's school, (b) I would develop a sense of deep satisfaction from helping others, and (c) I felt really, really guilty.

When I arrived at the book fair, the volunteer parent on the previous shift greeted me enthusiastically and quickly explained that all I needed to do was help the children find books, then ring up their purchases on the cash register.

"Don't worry, it's simple," she assured me. "Just press the red button to enter the price of the book, and the blue button for subtotals—unless they have more than two books and want to pay by check. Then use the yellow round one on the left. If you press the green square key the correct change will pop up on the screen, but only if they paid cash—not ATM or credit cards. See? Easy, huh?"

"No problem." I could handle money. After all, I'd been through college and had worked in a fast food restaurant before. Plus there was always the chance no one would buy anything.

My hopes were dashed when a group of elementary school children, dizzy with freedom and pockets full of change, burst through the door.

"Do you have any *Goosebumps* books here?" a little boy asked, "like the one about the giant, fire-breathing monster with laser eyes and bloody fangs that smashes cars with its bare feet?"

"No, I don't think so," I said looking through the shelves. "But how about this nice book about a talking duck who gets lost in the forest and is helped by a friendly little squirrel?"

"Forget it," he said, turning to his friend. "Jeez, whose mom is that, anyway?"

But it didn't matter what he thought. The most important thing was that I was taking the time to volunteer and support my children's school.

Fortunately, things starting going better since most of the other children left me alone—that is all except for the demanding few who kept insisting on buying books. Now I know what you're thinking, and I would gladly have rung up their purchases if I could've remembered the color scheme.

However, they didn't give up easily and before I knew it, a long line had formed in front of the register. I could sense the crowd was going to get ugly if I didn't do something fast.

So I did what any educated college graduate would do: I frantically tried pressing all of the buttons, hoping the right combination would either make the drawer fly open or set off the fire alarm so we could all evacuate the building and go home.

"That's not how you do it." A five-year-old girl reached over the register and pressed the red button. "See?"

She was obviously a future PTA president.

By the time the last child approached me, I was so tired I didn't even look up.

"Paper or plastic?" I said automatically. "Would you like some fries with that?"

But when he walked out the door happily carrying a bag full of new books, I realized that volunteering had given me a real sense of satisfaction after all—either that or it was the aftereffect from the adrenaline rush. But no matter what it was, I knew I would help the PTA again. I just hoped next time they'd give me something easier to do—like baking eighty-seven dozen cupcakes.

Fuzzy Bear's Great Adventure

The most popular member of my daughter's kindergarten classroom is Fuzzy Bear, a two-foot tall stuffed animal with matted fur, beady eyes, and a slightly dubious odor. He is raffled off on Fridays to pay a surprise visit to an unsuspecting family, who is supposed to record its weekend adventures with him in his portable journal.

The weekend my daughter won Fuzzy Bear, it took three trips to carry his luggage from the classroom into the car. He had a wardrobe larger than Ivana Trump. He had jeans for camping, pajamas for relaxing, suits for power lunches, and ski gear for weekends in Tahoe. He also had various gifts the children had given him: a miniature car (minus the wheels), three feet of train track (minus the train) and a plastic Tyrannosaurus Rex with a Malibu Barbie head.

"I hope he has coveralls and a tool belt," my husband said when we arrived home. "I plan on tuning up the car and repairing the roof this weekend."

My hopes were dashed. How were we supposed to have an exciting, adventurous family experience to write about if we didn't take a day trip? I knew by Monday the word would be out that my children spend their weekends in their slippers in front of the TV and are as stimulated as a pack of hibernating stump slugs.

I quickly found the journal and began scanning the pages to see what Fuzzy Bear did with other families.

According to the journal, the McGlory family went scuba diving off the California coast and discovered a wrecked Spanish galleon containing sunken treasure. The Looneys went camping for two days in the wilderness and taught Fuzzy Bear how to gut a fish and build a campfire with two sticks. The Kraftys watched the migration of the whales and created a papier-mâché replica of an orca in their garage. Nowhere did it say Fuzzy Bear stayed in his pajamas all weekend and watched 48 consecutive hours of cartoons. It was obvious Fuzzy was a high maintenance bear.

I was determined for my children and I to have something wonderful to write about, so at dawn on Saturday morning, we dressed Fuzzy in a nautical outfit and went garage "sailing." We explored unfamiliar neighborhoods, watched the sun rise above a velvet painting of Elvis, and felt the wind whip at our backs as we searched strange driveways for the perfect deal.

After mooring the car at home for lunch, we changed Fuzzy into hiking boots and camouflage fatigues and took a nature walk down the driveway to the mailbox.

"Let's see how many plants and animals we can observe," I said. We found two leaves (that hadn't blow away yet), several ants on an old soda can in the gutter, and the neighbor's cat. We glued the leaves to a piece of binder paper and stuck it on the refrigerator.

When we recovered from all of the fresh air, my daughter announced she wanted to go camping. So we tossed blankets and pillows on the lawn furniture in the backyard. We roasted marshmallows over the gas grill and read stories by the glow of the porch light. The kids fell asleep while my husband was still trying to find the Big Dipper.

The next morning we went on a safari to the wilds of the neighborhood grocery store to buy breakfast. We observed live lobsters splashing in the tank, and fought off a band of vultures trying to steal our cart while we sampled a new jelly flavor on a cracker.

When we got home, my children unpacked Fuzzy's wardrobe and were entertained for hours. One moment he was dressed as a police bear in a dark blue suit and badge, the next he was a pirate bear with an eye patch and scarf. Then, when my daughter decided to dress him in her old doll's clothes, he became a transvestite bear with a lace apron and a string of plastic pearls.

In the evening, I gathered the children on my lap and opened the journal. I wrote:

Dear Journal,

The Farmer family is incredible! I sailed at sunrise and communed with nature. I camped under the stars and went on a safari to an

exciting and hostile place. I learned how to collect samples of wildlife and preserve them. My weekend was nonstop fun and excitement!
Love,
Fuzzy B.

P.S. The television wasn't turned on once and no one sat on the sofa and ate chips for breakfast in their pajamas.

I snapped the journal closed and gently moved my children who were fast asleep. I went into the kitchen, pulled the leaf picture off the front of the refrigerator, and added it to Fuzzy Bear's luggage to thank him for the wonderful weekend he gave my family.

Fifth Grade Parent Volunteer

Year after year, without exception, I've helped out in my child's classroom. During my career as a parent volunteer I've cut out zillions of bunny patterns, assisted with countless finger painting projects, and even worked with a reading group or two.

But this year things are different. Very different. You see, now my daughter is in the fifth grade. Let me explain.

The first big difference I discovered about going into a fifth grade classroom is that there are a lot of new rules that I must follow, most of which are made up by my daughter. Some of the basic tenets are: 1) do not wave or make eye contact with any other human being in the room, 2) do not say things like "by golly," "gee whiz," or "groovy," 3) do not tell stories from anyone's sordid past as a baby, and 4) do not, under any circumstances, wear the flowered leggings with the wide-brimmed straw hat because "it's not the 80's anymore, you know."

The other important difference is that there will be no paintbrushes or fluffy bunny patterns waiting for you to cut out. Nooooo. Chances are, there will be nothing but a lot of serious learning going on there.

Take the other day, for instance. As soon as I arrived, the teacher steered me to the back table and explained to me that I was to (ha, ha) supervise a few students who needed to finish a pre-algebra math page. "Just help them if they have any questions," he said. Then he mumbled something about square roots and commutative property and, I think, the formula to the creation of the universe as he calmly sauntered away, leaving me with nothing but my wits on which to survive.

Now don't get me wrong. I'm a big fan of math. It comes in handy in all sorts of important situations: like figuring out how much the beige Versace handbag you had your eye on will cost after it finally goes on sale for 40% off. But truth be told, as far as any kind of advanced math goes, I am sorely lacking. I'm the type of person who firmly believes that the letter "x" belongs in words, and has absolutely no business whatsoever hanging around in math problems.

Life being what it is, no sooner had I begun to relax than a girl raised her hand and pointed to a long string of numbers, letters and fractions that looked like some kind of Martian secret code.

"Can you help me?" she asked.

I immediately flashed back to the last time I tried balancing the checkbook.

"Well, you see," I said, "you take this number and move it over here, then you times it by the amount you think it should be, then subtract, oh say, $57.00, then you take a wild guess and call the bank. Easy, eh?"

But it was no good. I could tell by the kind of look she gave me that she could see right through my flimsy charade.

However, the very second I stopped speaking something peculiar happened: memories of my fifth grade year came flooding back. Granted it also brought up the words to Staying Alive, the Hustle, and all the names of the Bee Gees. But pre-algebra was mixed in there somewhere, too.

Sure, I'd like to say everything was different after that. That we all spent the rest of the afternoon sitting at the back table discussing calculus and revising the theory of time-space continuum and all that. But we didn't. The kids quietly finished their math papers then went back to their seats and I went on my way, pining for the good old days of finger painting stations and reading centers.

Things were so happy and innocent then.

A Kindergartner's Rules for Life

As I watched the twenty-four members of my son's preschool class proudly hitch up their good pants and walk out onto the stage to receive their diplomas, I could hardly believe my eyes. It seemed like only yesterday they were squishing clay through their hands or finger-painting or figuring out the mystery of putting on their own socks. Now they were graduating. *Graduating!*

When the ceremony began, the teacher solemnly led the preschool class of 2000 in a rousing rendition of "Five Little Fishies," complete with finger movements. This was followed by "I am a Nut" and an unidentifiable rhyming song that had something to do with a giraffe, although I'm not sure what.

After they received their diplomas, we followed the alumnus into the classroom to celebrate their accomplishments by eating cake and ice cream.

All in all, it was a wonderful ceremony. But afterwards, when the glow of the excitement had worn off, I began thinking about how, in a matter of weeks, my son would be moving from the safe, familiar world of preschool to the unknown, confusing world of kindergarten.

Of course I had prepared him the best I could, but what does someone who has never left the front yard by himself really know about life?

So in case I'm ever asked to give a commencement address for a preschool graduation, I've created a list of all the important rules every five-year-old should know:

Don't be afraid to ask where the restroom is.

Always put on your pants before you put on your shoes.

When using scissors, make sure you point them away from your good shirt.

Flush.

Wear your jacket outside on a cold day even, if it covers up your Batman cape.

It doesn't matter where you stand in line as long as you're in it.

Don't bother mixing purple and orange paint.

No matter what anyone tells you, you will never be left at school to fend for yourself after all of the other children have gone home.

The kitchen area isn't just for girls.

Never call anyone a booger-nose. And don't trust anyone who calls you a booger-nose, then breaks your new set of crayons on purpose.

If you're wearing a new belt, don't wait until the last minute to head for the restroom.

Never trade your milk money for an extra turn on the tricycle.

Be nice to people who are bigger than you—for obvious reasons. Be nice to people who are smaller than you because one day they may be bigger.

Share.

Don't eat crackers with wet hands.

Wait patiently for your turn.

Sing and dance and learn. Then dance some more, but only if it's okay with your teacher.

Try not to smear your nametag on the first day of school.

At recess, make the big kid standing behind you go down the slide first.

Never choose something just because it's shiny.

Don't get put in the time-out chair for breaking the same rule twice.

Color in the lines.

Ask for a Kleenex instead of wiping your nose on the back of your hand.

When in doubt, raise your hand.

Don't lick your glue stick.

Always say "please" and "thank you," even if you're not sure what for.

Don't spit in the water fountain.

On the first day of school, cry a little bit just for your parent's sake.

And, most importantly, give your parents a kiss good-bye. They'll need it.

THERE'S NO ONE QUITE LIKE DEAR OL' DAD

A Father's View

I hate to be stereotypical, but let's face it; mothers view parenthood differently than fathers. For example, the minute a woman knows she's pregnant she starts buying books with titles like, *The Perfect Parent*, and meticulously studies every word until she becomes a new baby expert. Now this may not seem so bad, but at the end of nine months she casually tosses around words like "pabulum" and "meconium" in mixed company, and she is absolutely sure her baby will be born with every incurable disease discovered in the entire world—possibly the universe.

On top of that, once the baby is born she will recite the length and duration of every labor pain, the amount of medication administered during labor and every word the doctor spoke in the delivery room. Fathers, on the other hand, remember the entire birth experience as the day he spent fifteen minutes trying to find a convenient place to park.

Oh, before you start yelling, I know that this doesn't apply to all fathers. Some block out the whole experience altogether. But that's okay. A father's real job comes later.

For instance, when a baby has colic, a mother immediately thinks that all of the doctors are wrong and it must be due to some horrible disease that hasn't been discovered yet because she is sure no normal person in this world could ever cry so much, and she'd give anything for it to stop, but she's sure she'll never get any sleep for another eighteen years because that's when the baby will finally stop crying and go off on its own to college.

A father will think, "The baby is hungry."

But that's not all. When most mothers are spending hours scanning catalogs deciding what type of stroller to buy, a father will save time by buying one big stroller that's more like a giant Swiss Army knife. While mothers are wasting valuable naptime doing research, fathers are busy converting high chairs into swings, car seats into potty-chairs and strollers into television sets.

But wait, there's more. While most mothers are teaching their children valuable life skills, like how to use a potty or hold a spoon properly, fathers are teaching important skills like how to catapult peas across the room with a fork during dinner.

Mothers also keep meticulous records of things, like the date of a baby's first step and first intelligible words. They maintain scrapbooks full of pictures, snippets of hair, baby's first booties and all that. Fathers keep one badly worn picture in their wallet.

When a mother takes a baby to the park, she brings all of the essential items she would ordinarily need to go on a short outing to, say, Australia. Fathers, on the other hand, are ready to leave the house in two minutes flat with one spare diaper tucked into their back pocket and a baby backpack that converts into a swing.

I'm not sure why this happens. I mean, who can really explain, when a child is learning to walk, why some mothers line the entire house with Styrofoam and spend the day following their toddler around with both arms outstretched, while a father will set a toddler on the top of a bike ramp propped in the backyard, flash them a thumbs up sign, and shout, "Ready, set, go!"

Some people think men have a more relaxed attitude because they were raised differently than women. Still others say that it's all a matter of individual parenting styles. My theory—and frankly I can't get anyone to back this up—is that fathers take more risks because they still have their pre-pregnancy figures. But I could be wrong about this.

However, I'm sure about one thing: even though men might have a different view of parenthood, there's no one quite like a father.

Handy Dad

I knew my husband was in the first stage of a mid-life crisis when he developed a fantasy that he was capable of handling all of the household repairs. Suddenly a reasonable man, who can barely tie his shoes or change a light bulb without causing a blackout in three states, decided money shouldn't be squandered on overpriced, incompetent professionals.

At first I played along with his fantasy, hoping it would go away. This tactic worked fine until my bathroom sink began to leak.

"Don't bother calling the plumber," my husband called, strapping on his tool belt. "It's only a little drip."

By noon, the "little drip" turned into Niagara Falls and the drain was plugged by my husband's screwdriver. My children thought we'd installed an indoor pool.

"Maybe we should call the plumber," I said, "before the Sierra Club declares our house a protected national wetland and we can't get in to use the bathroom."

"Very funny," he said, looking out from under the sink. "I'm almost finished."

"Finished? I need a snorkel and a pair of fins to take a shower and I see a group of spawning salmon migrating this way."

I finally called the plumber that evening, after my husband fell asleep on the sofa clutching the plunger. He charged seventy-five dollars to come out at night to wade down my hall, pry out the screwdriver, and replace a fifty-cent washer.

At Christmas time my husband refused to pay the extra assembly fee for the children's presents and insisted on putting them together himself. It took him seventeen evenings in the garage and he used every power tool we had in the house, including the can opener. The day before Christmas Eve he ushered me out into the garage after the children went to sleep. I stared in horror. My son's bike looked like it had been rear ended by a Barbie house and the Big Wheel looked like a Picasso. The next day I rushed the toys back to the store and paid an employee an extra fee to detach and reassemble the toys in time for Christmas.

Things improved until the day the washing machine sounded like an air raid siren preceding a hostile missile attack. I hoped my husband wouldn't notice until the repairman was on his way.

"What noise?" I screamed into his ear. "I don't hear anything except the chirping of baby birds and the tranquil voices of children playing!"

It didn't work. He scoured the house trying to find the toolbox I hid under a juniper bush in the backyard.

He gave up and grabbed a flashlight, a plastic wrench from my son's tool set, and a butter knife.

When the sound stopped my son rushed from the laundry room yelling, "Monster eat Daddy!" and I perused the sales in the paper for a new machine.

The weekend after the new machine was installed I caught my husband in the garage trying to jack up the car.

"Stop!" I cried, throwing myself over the hood. "What are you doing?"

"It's time to change the oil," he said. "I'm sick of taking it to an overpriced garage when I can do it myself."

"The only thing you've ever changed in the car is the clock," I said. "Let me take care of it."

"You think I'm incompetent," he accused.

"No, but since you've take over the repairs, we're broke."

His shoulders drooped.

"It's okay." I put my arm around him and led him into the house. "Just let me organize the repairs and *you* stick with what you know."

We were interrupted by a noise in the backyard. We went out and our youngest son was running towards us sobbing.

"Owie." He ran past me and held out his arm, "Daddy fix."

My husband kissed the sore spot on his hand and gave him a hug. The crying stopped and as they went into the house to get a bandage and a glass of lemonade, I realized my husband was a gifted handyman who repaired more important things than faucets.

Father's Day Isn't Just For Anybody

It's for the father who spends three weekends in the garage trying to assemble a new bike with nothing but a wrench and a butter knife, and for the father who pays extra to have any toy that comes in more than two pieces assembled before leaving the store.

It's for the father who takes the family camping for a week to "rough it" with nothing but a few sleeping bags and a Swiss Army knife, and for the father who thinks "roughing it" is spending the night in a discount hotel without cable TV.

It's for the father who spends Saturday afternoon coaching his child's little league team, and for the father who spends Saturday afternoon cheering on his child's little league team.

It's for the father who takes the family on long bike rides around the neighborhood, and for the father whose only exercise is pushing the buttons on a video game.

It's for the father who builds a fort in the back yard with lumber and power tools, and for the father who builds one using two cardboard boxes and duct tape.

It's for the father who helps his children brush their teeth before going to bed, and the father who teaches them how to rinse by spitting out water between their two front teeth like a fountain.

It's for the father who can change the oil, spark plugs, and tires on the family car like a mechanic at Indianapolis 500, and for the father who has trouble changing the time on the dashboard clock.

It's for the father who scrubs his children each night during bath time, and for the father who teaches his children how to catapult the soap into the sink with the washcloth.

It's for the father who knows where he's going before he gets in the car for a family outing, and for the father who doesn't need directions because he knows his destination is "somewhere around here."

It's for the father who gives his child five dollars for a tooth he spent an hour trying to pull out with a string, and for the father who tries to reuse the bath water to save money.

It's for the father who puts up the Christmas lights by November and takes them down by January first, and for the father who never puts lights up because the last time he saw the ladder, it was propping up the back end of the car while he changed the tire.

It's for the father who goes into the wilderness, skewers a worm on a hook, reels in a fish, and cooks it over an open flame on a piece of tin foil, and for the father who needs a welding torch and a bucket of kerosene to light the briquettes in the barbecue.

It's for fathers who are tall, short, rich, poor, generous, cheap, married, divorced, mustached, bearded or bald.

It's for every father who loves his children.

Remotely Controlled

The words, "Honey, I just bought a universal remote," have probably been responsible for more divorces than mid-life crisis or infidelity. The night my husband came home and spoke those words, I knew the little bit of control I had over my life would soon be gone.

"You're going to love this," he assured me. "We're going to be a one-remote family. No more digging around under the furniture to change the station. The television, VCR, and stereo system will be hooked together and at your finger tips."

"But when will I clean out the sofa?" I said. "The last time I lost the remote under the cushions I found a pretzel with more hair than Jerry Garcia, ten dollars in Confederate money, and a mood ring."

Besides, with three remotes I always knew where I stood. I color-coded each one with a wad of chewed bubble gum so I'd know at a glance which one I needed. The television was Godzilla Grape, the VCR Bazooka Blue, and the stereo was Passion fruit Pink.

I watched my husband disconnect our electronic equipment and struggle on the living room floor in the middle of a mass of tangled cords and cables like a humongous spider weaving a big, black universally-controlled web. Several hours later he handed me the remote.

"Okay, working it is simple," he said. "The red button turns on the television and the stereo, the blue button starts the VCR with the TV, and the yellow button turns on the VCR with the stereo, but only if the stereo is off and the timer is set. See? Easy, huh?"

I felt as if Einstein had just recited the theory of relativity to me, in Pig Latin backwards. The only thing I knew for sure was that I needed new gum colors. I figured I'd work with it tomorrow after he went to work.

The next day I assembled my children in the living room for a dose of educational programming while I finished chores around the house. I reached for the remote, then pointed and clicked. Nothing. I waved the remote towards the television and stood on one foot. Nothing. I fell on my knees and pleaded. Nothing. I offered it money, jewels, and a cruise to the Bahamas in the spring. Still nothing.

I sat down and tried to remember my husband's color-coded instructions, but I was lost without purple—it had always started the television before. I tried pressing the red and blue buttons simultaneously and the garage door opened, the dryer started, and the toilet flushed in the downstairs bathroom—but the television didn't flicker.

I didn't give up. I kept pressing colored buttons until we were watching Barney, but listening to the Rolling Stones.

"Cool," my daughter said. "What's 'satisfaction?'"

I snapped everything off. "Let's go outside and play." I figured we could survive eight hours without the television until my husband came home. Things were going great until it began to rain. By mid-afternoon, we'd put together every puzzle in the house and colored on every piece of paper I had, including the *TV Guide*.

I herded my family back into the living room and grasped the remote. I held it to my lips, said a short prayer, aimed, and pressed. Suddenly, there was a picture on the screen with matching words. My children applauded.

"Hurry kids," I said, "I'm not sure how long this will last."

We gathered on the sofa and watched an episode of *Animal Planet* because it was educational (and I was afraid of turning on a hostile appliance while trying to change the channel).

We were enthralled by a herd of sea lions beached on an island in Argentina. This would've been a great learning experience if it hadn't been mating season. I hoped my children wouldn't notice.

"Why is the big one hurting the baby?"

"It's not the baby. It's the mommy." I frantically pressed the clicker, then threw my body in front of the screen when nothing happened. "It's just a game—like football."

Finally the sea lion segment ended and we moved on to the next animal. I began to sob during the "Life of Anthropoids."

"What's wrong, Mommy?" my children asked.

"I just want to change the channel without turning on the garbage disposal." I said. "I want the television on when I press a button and Mick Jagger off. I want to listen to music without having to earn a Ph.D. in engineering from Harvard. I want some control back in my life!"

My children stared at me until my three-year-old son broke the silence. "Music?" he said as he gently took the remote from my hand, turned off the TV and put his Barney sing-a-long tape in the cassette player. Then he pressed play, adjusted the eight knobs on the equalizer, and balanced the speakers.

I watched in amazement and wondered how long it would take my husband to find the universal remote if I stuffed it under the sofa cushions, behind my collection of furry cheese sticks.

☆de to Dad

A father's job is unique. If parents had job descriptions mine would read: organize bills, play dates, laundry, meals, laundry, carpool, laundry, snacks, outings, and laundry. The only thing on my husband's description would be the word "fun" written in big red letters along the top. Although he is a selfless caregiver and provider, our children think of him more as a combination jungle gym and Bozo the clown.

Our parenting styles compliment each other. His style is a nonstop adventure where no one has to worry about washing their hands, eating vegetables, or getting cavities. My style is similar to Mussolini. I'm too busy worrying to be fun. Besides, every time I try, my husband constantly outdoes me.

I bought my children bubble gum flavored toothpaste and I taught them how to brush their teeth in tiny circles so they wouldn't get cavities. They thought it was neat until my husband taught them how to rinse by spitting out water between their two front teeth.

I tried singing fun songs as I scrubbed behind my children's ears during bath time. They enthusiastically sang and clapped until their father came in and taught them how to catapult soap into the sink with a washcloth.

I took the children on a nature walk and after two hours, I managed to corral a slow ladybug into my son's insect cage. I was "cool" until their father came home, spent two minutes in the backyard, and captured a beetle the size of a Chihuahua.

I try to tell myself I'm a good parent even if my husband does things I can't do. I can make sure my children are safe, warm, and dry. I'll stand in line for five hours so the children can see Santa at the mall—or be first in line to see the latest Disney movie where I'll spend more than my monthly mortgage payment on a bucket of popcorn and a soda. But I can't wire the VCR so my children can watch their favorite video.

I can carry my children in my arms when they're tired, tuck them into bed, and kiss them goodnight. But I can't flip them upside down so they can walk on the ceiling or prop them on my shoulders so they can see the moths flying around inside the light fixture.

I can take them to doctor appointments, scout meetings, or field trips to the aquarium; but I'll never go into the wilderness, skewer a worm on a hook, reel in a fish and then cook it over an open flame on a piece of tin foil.

I'll even sit in the first row of every little league game and cheer until my throat is sore and my tonsils are raw, but I'll never teach my son how to hit a home run or slide into first base.

As a mother I can do a lot of things for my children, but no matter how hard I try—I can never be their father.

A Real Swinger

I sensed trouble the day my husband returned from the store with a stack of boards, a plastic slide, and two swings laying in the back of his truck.

"I bought a wooden play structure for the kids," he said. "They're gonna love it!"

"But . . ."

"Don't worry," he said. "We can afford it. I decided to put it together myself to save money."

I nodded and wondered how my husband could build a twenty-foot wooden structure when the only tool he knew how to use was duct tape.

"Are you sure you can handle it?" I asked.

"Of course," he said. "All I need to do is follow the directions. Besides, I made a wooden shelf in my high school shop class."

My husband spent the first day dragging all of the planks from the truck to the backyard. At dinnertime I found him outside studying the directions and mumbling to himself.

"I can do this with my eyes closed," he said. "By the way, do we have a butter knife?"

The next day he leveled the ground and moved the planks around the yard while our children watched anxiously.

"Are you almost finished, Daddy?" my daughter asked.

"It's coming right along." He kneeled down and bolted a few pieces of wood loosely together.

"Cool," my daughter said. "A see-saw."

As my husband progressed, I began to notice various household items disappearing.

"Have you seen the bread maker?" I asked.

"Yeah, I needed something sturdy to lean against the backside of the clubhouse while I bolted it down," he said.

"What about the electric broom?"

"It's propping up the rope ladder until I can fasten it on."

"The vacuum?"

"It's holding up the slide."

"Call me naïve, but I don't think that's in the directions."

"Well, of course not," he said. "Whoever wrote them obviously didn't know what they were doing." He stepped over the bread maker and adjusted the broom handle. "Plus the kit is missing some parts, so I had to improvise."

"Are you almost finished?" my daughter asked.

"Of course," he said, "just as soon as I attach the blue thingy to the wood what-cha-ma-call-it with the metal bally whacker."

Two weeks later he called us out to the backyard to see the finished play structure.

"See?" he said. "I told you I knew what I was doing."

I was impressed. From a distance it looked great. But as I got closer, I noticed the rope ladder dangled over the sandbox, the tire swing hung at a jaunty angle to the left, the slide was held in place by the garden hose, and the monkey bars were bolted to the outside wall of the clubhouse.

"Yippee!" my son cried. "A fire truck!"

I couldn't bring myself to say anything since my husband had worked so hard and our children obviously loved it. Besides, I figured as soon as they were tired of it I could plant wisteria in the sandbox, remove the slide and swings, attach a trellis onto the hanging rope and put a bench in the clubhouse— and I'd have one heck of a gazebo.

Father-Child Events

The one thing I've learned about life, being a mother all these years, is that you've got to watch out for any event trying to pass itself off as "father-child" activity. Not that there's anything wrong with a father spending time with his children. But what no one tells you is that there is really no such thing as a father-child activity. Any fool knows it's really a secret code meaning *mother-child* activity—without the mother, of course. Now before you start thinking this is going to be just another stereotypical male bashing type of story, it isn't. I'm strictly speaking from personal experience.

And, mind you, nothing speaks louder than our involvement with the local Indian Guide troop.

The Indian Guides, for those of you who don't know, is a group of fathers and sons similar to Boy Scouts, who meet once a month at various members' houses for a discussion, crafts, and a snack. But the real beauty of it is that fathers are supposed organize everything, EVERYTHING! The mother's only involvement is to stand on the front porch waving to the father and son as they drive off down the cul-de-sac for the monthly meeting.

At least that's what I thought until our annual Indian Guide Troop potluck picnic.

Now you're probably thinking that a group of eight men arranging a day at the park with their families sounds like a fun, family bonding experience. And you're right.

However, there was one particular drawback that hadn't occurred to me: there is very a big difference on how men and women plan picnics. I mean actual scientific studies have proven this. For instance, most women will spend hours debating the best day and exact starting time, then activate a phone-tree to decide what type of theme to have, whether to serve beef or chicken and who, exactly can be trusted to bring the hotdog buns and potato salad. Men will discuss the whole event for about, say, five minutes and decide on the location of the park.

Now, granted, some of you out there (and you know who you are) are pounding your fist on the table, shouting, "Hey, that's nothing but a stereotypical exaggeration! Besides, location is *important*, you know?"

This brings up a whole new set of problems; one being that it bases the whole picnic planning process loosely on rumor. Out of eight families, two thought it was "some time during Saturday," two "late on Sunday," and the rest were evenly divided (although they were absolutely sure they were in charge of bringing the ice).

Now the other problem with father-child activities is that most men don't admit they need any help until five, maybe six minutes before the start of an event. And yes, while this may be another flaming generalization, it surely explains why my friend Carol called me on her cell phone from a local discount store the other day, panic-stricken because a group of sixteen fathers and sons was supposed to meet at her house at six.

"Hi, it's me," she panted. "What aisle are the popsicle sticks on?"

"What?"

"We're weaving 'God's Eyes' at the meeting tonight."

"Try aisle two."

"What about the yarn?"

"Seven."

"Thanks. Gotta run!"

Clearly, I don't have to tell you what's going on here. Left to their own devices, most fathers would be wandering around Popsicle-stickless, having no idea when to meet at the park.

But on the other hand, let's face it, without them there'd be no high-speed cable connections or fancy remote control satellite television systems. Okay, maybe there would be, but most of them wouldn't be connected right.

I must admit, however, father-child activities have taught me one thing: no matter how hard you try, you can't change a person's nature.

So now, whenever my husband announces that he's going on a father-son camping trip or a father-daughter hike, I just smile weakly and say, "That's nice, dear. It sounds like fun."

Then I dash for the phone, call the other mothers in the troop to set up the day and time, air out the sleeping bags, pull down the suitcases, make a list of clothing they'll need, fill the water bottles, and pack up all of the snacks.

It's just easier that way.

Husband Speak

My husband just got off the phone with his old friend, Vini. Now granted, this might not seem like such a big deal to you; however, Vini isn't just any friend. Nooooo. Vini is my husband's very best, through-thick-and-thin type pal from high school whom he hasn't heard from in years. *Years!*

So when he hung up it seemed perfectly reasonable that I ask, "How's Vini?"

"Who?" He said. "Oh, yeah. Fine."

"Well?" I said. "How are the kids? Is he still living in the same house?

"I guess so."

"Where does he work? Is he still married?"

"Uh, well, I dunno."

"Then what in the heck did you talk about for an hour?"

"Computers," he said in an "of course" kind of way. "He has a new 286 PC and needed advice on hooking it up."

Now, that's just the kind of thing you can expect from a man. They can talk for hours to their very best friend, the very person with whom they were soul mates during their high school years mind you, and not get any good information at all.

Frankly, I should've expected this. The same thing happened the time my husband was invited over by a nationally known rock band to fix their computer system. Now, I don't know about you, but this is the sort of thing that qualifies for my "Fantasy Island Material Category," right along with fitting in size seven jeans and finding trendy tennis shoes for 75% off.

So naturally, I couldn't wait for him to return home to tell me all of the details.

"Well, how'd it go?" I asked, jumping to my feet the second he walked through the door.

"Fine."

"FINE?" I cried. "What did their house look like? How did they dress? Did they have a sofa or futons? Real art or posters?"

He shrugged.

"For gosh sakes," I clutched his coat lapels in my fists. "Give me some information! Anything!" I pleaded.

"I don't remember," he said. "Oh yeah. They had a really nice big screen television."

Now I don't need to tell you that this sort of thing doesn't happen with women.

For instance, just the other day I called up the JC Penny catalog department to order a set of ceramic table lamps for the living room.

"Yes, I need two of number 546-A in beige," I said over the phone to the nice catalog operator named Mary. "But I need to make sure they'll go with a white leather sofa and olive curtains. What do you think?"

"Well, if I were you," she paused, "I'd stick with 535-B, the brass floor lamp."

"Oh?"

"At least that's what I have in my house. And it looks fabulous, especially since I have Pergo flooring.

"Hey! Me, too!"

By the time I finished, I knew the color of Mary's kitchen, how long she'd been married, the names and ages of her children, and that her oldest child, a high school senior, just got a soccer scholarship to Colorado State, but is thinking about going to Julliard to study musical composition instead.

Truth be told, if she hadn't been in another state, we probably would've made plans to go shopping and out to lunch the following Saturday.

"What was that all about?" my husband asked after I hung up the phone.

"Oh, nothing. I was just buying some lamps."

He looked at me as if I was insane or something.

But then again, what can you expect from someone who orders take-out Chinese food by blurting "Number 51" into the telephone and hanging up?

Not that there's anything wrong with that.

But, between you and me, I can't imagine going through life that way. I mean, if I did, I'd never have gotten to know my friend Gloria at the bank, who has six cats and is thinking of quitting her job and becoming a midwife; or Rosie at the grocery store, who went to the Oscars because she has a brother who's a professional movie extra.

Now some people might think I'm just being nosey, but I consider it more as being a "detective of human interest."

That said, I guess there will always be some things that will remain a mystery to me. Like, for example, how Vini is doing.

Unless I call his wife, of course, whoever she may be.

Much More Than i Need To Know

✪ut of Touch

Have you noticed that lately there's been an alarming increase in the amount of people talking on cell phones in public places? It seems to me that nowadays a person can't venture anywhere without hearing half of a private conversation. And mind you, it's not just conversations. People are doing all sorts of shocking things in public: like making business deals, discussing custody arrangements, gossiping and making tawdry weekend plans.

Oh, relax, it's not like I'm listening. But how can you ignore a man standing behind you at the gas station who's loudly describing all the details of his office romance? Or a woman in the produce section of the grocery store who is clutching a cell phone to her ear and quietly sobbing into the Portobello mushrooms? This just seems wrong.

But the real reason I resent people taking up my peaceful air space with their lively, animated conversations is that they somehow look more important than the rest of us. It might be because of the way they disregard society's rules by laughing and talking in normally quiet places. Or perhaps it's because of the way they inadvertently let the rest of the world know they have a life. Or maybe, just maybe, it's because they can say things like, "Hey, baby, I just wanted to tell you how much I love your sexy smile," in the middle of the frozen food aisle and get away with it.

So I decided to do something I vowed I would never do: I took my cell phone out of the glove compartment (where I keep it only for emergencies), upped my monthly service plan, and handed out my cell phone number to everyone I know.

Soon I, too, would be vivaciously tossing my head back, making plans out loud in public, and broadcasting to the world that I am both important and mysterious.

However, I had to wait longer than I thought since the first time the phone rang I was trying on a bathing suit in a dressing room at the local department store and by the time I had covered myself up sufficiently to answer the phone, it stopped ringing.

Fortunately, the second time it rang my luck changed and I was in line at a crowded, upscale boutique.

I held the phone to my ear at a jaunty angle, threw my head back, and said, "Hello?" in a sultry voice.

"Mom?" my five-year-old son said. "Where are my soccer cleats?"

"What? I can't hear you."

"I can't find my soccer cleats!"

"Oh, why didn't you say so," I laughed loudly. "Hors d'oeuvres at eight sounds great."

"Mom?"

I quickly looked around and cupped my hand over the receiver. "They're in the upstairs bathroom on the hamper," I whispered.

"Thanks, Mom."

"See you later!" I said, and hung up.

Just as I was paying for my purchases it rang again.

"Excuse me for a moment," I said to the clerk as I whipped open my phone. "Hello?"

"Can I have a Pepsi?"

"I'm sorry I can't today. I'm simply booked," I said loudly. Then I turned sideways and hissed "No!" into the phone and threw it back into my purse.

I made it all the way to the parking lot before it rang again.

"What!" I snapped.

"They're not on the hamper."

"Where's your father!"

"He's busy, but he said it was okay to call you now since you have a phone."

This was followed by a call from my daughter crying about a lost ladybug named Cindy and two more from my son tattling on his sister for calling him a booger-nose.

All in all, I received sixteen calls in two days and none of them from anyone with a full set of permanent teeth. Now, I know what you're thinking. You're thinking that any fool with children would've seen this coming. And you're right. I bet they would have seen my bill coming, too: $234.57. This is the trouble with cell phones.

So I did the only reasonable thing I could think of: I turned the phone off and tossed it back into the glove compartment. After all, why should I pay for the convenience of solving problems and breaking up fights long distance when I can stay home and do it for free?

ℳaking It Up

There are two kinds of women who apply their own make-up: those who emerge from their boudoir each morning looking polished and sophisticated and those like me who spend most of their adult years ping-ponging between the natural look and that of the raccoon family—and never quite getting it right.

So for my thirtieth birthday, I decided to get a complimentary makeover at one of those chic department stores that sells expensive perfumes and imported leather bags.

I sat down in an empty chair next to several brands of make-up that I couldn't pronounce and tried to explain to the eighteen-year-old beauty consultant what I wanted.

"I want bigger eyes, more cheek bones and less chin," I said, trying to demonstrate with my hands. "You know, kind of like a young Farrah Fawcett."

"Who?" she said.

"Never mind."

She handed me a mirror and I held it face-up on my lap as she cleaned off my old make-up and applied liquid foundation to even out my skin. As she worked, I began to relax. Soon, I would rise above being the type of person who puts on mascara at red lights during the car pool and lifted into the ranks of a sophisticated woman who looks as if she just emerged from a Vogue photo shoot and is on her way to a charity function at the Ritz Carlton.

Then the consultant showed me a palette of eye shadow colors. "What colors do you like?"

Now, even though I've never had this done, I had a hunch this was something that she was supposed to tell me.

I suppressed the urge to blurt out, "Do you think I'd be walking around like *this* if I knew what looked good?" But instead, I obediently looked at the colors.

Now normally, my first choice would be a nice combination of burgundy red and hunter green. But since those colors look best on, say, ottomans, I scanned the palette for a second choice.

I finally chose gold and beige since they were nice, neutral shades. I waited patiently while she slathered several coats onto my lids.

Next I chose a black eyeliner pencil. But since I'm always a little bit leery when someone is coming towards my eye with a sharp object, I couldn't sit still while she applied it.

"Let me show you how I do it," I said finally, taking the eyeliner out of her hand.

When I finished accenting my eyes, she handed me several lipsticks to choose from. After much deliberation, I finally chose a festive auburn color that looked great on the stick. As she applied it, I imagined my thin lips becoming luscious, full, and pouty—sort of a cross between Drew Barrymore and Mick Jagger.

But when I looked into the mirror, I was shocked to see that my normally demure, translucent lips were now bright orange and protruding out of my face like the smiling yarn mouth on a monkey sock puppet.

"What do you think?" she asked, brushing vibrant red rouge on either cheek.

As I looked into the mirror I couldn't help thinking that my new make-up might look better on someone else—like, say, a cast member of the Rocky Horror picture show—than on a suburban mother-of-two. So I did the only thing I could: I whipped out the tube of lipstick I kept in my purse.

"Do you have something in this color?" I asked.

She shook her head, so I opened the tube and applied my own lipstick. Then I rubbed off some of the eye shadow with my fingers and grabbed a tissue and swiped at the blush on my cheeks until I'd reduced it to my usual muted rose tone.

"There," I said, blotting the liquid foundation with translucent powder from the compact I kept in my purse. "Perfect."

And as I gazed at my reflection in the mirror, I calculated that it would cost me about three times as much to have the same look I'd had when I left the house that morning. Naturally, the only wise and prudent thing to do was to stick with the make up I already had. But somehow this just felt wrong. So to make myself feel better, I bought a tube of twenty-dollar clear lip-gloss and stuck it in my purse.

Sometimes it's just better that way.

All in the Cards

One of my greatest fears has been realized: my grocery store club card is recording my every purchase. I have a feeling that somewhere in a corporate office, a team of marketing analysts is staring at a screen full of my personal consumer information thinking, "Good grief, this woman can't cook!"

Normally I'm not a paranoid person, but I'm not sure I like complete strangers knowing that the only fruit my family eats is the kind rolled up in a box and that I actually buy Spam. After all, what are they doing with this information? What if I'm sorted into a special bad mommy group that they're studying for future side effects from processed mystery food? What if my dentist finds out that each week I buy the sugarcoated cereal with the best prize in the box? Or what if, for gosh sakes, word gets out that in a moment of weakness, I bought a magazine with a cover story about a surrogate mother who gave birth to alien triplets?

I can imagine myself standing in the check-out line one day and just as soon as the cashier swipes my club card through the register, an alarm goes off and several police officers resembling Martha Stewart surround my cart, seize all of my boxes of frozen waffles and cheese whiz, and declare me an unfit mother.

I was so upset I had to call my friend Julie to see what she thought about this unfair invasion of consumer privacy.

"I don't see what you're getting all worked up about," she said. "It's just a discount card."

"That's easy for you to say." But what could I expect from a woman who bakes bread and makes her own meatballs?

So I did the only thing I could think of: buy food that would throw the consumer analysts off my trail.

The next time I went shopping I filled my basket with tofu and several other unidentifiable items in the organic produce section. I tossed in a giant root that looked like something out of a B-grade horror movie and a suspicious leafy green vegetable that I wasn't completely sure was legal.

When I finished, I proudly handed the cashier my card. "Starting today," I said loudly, "no one can accuse me of serving frozen pizza and Jujubes for dinner, no-siree!"

In fact, no one could accuse me of serving anything for dinner at all since I had no idea how to prepare any of the food I bought. As I struggled to create some kind of an edible meal, I decided it would be much easier to get a new card under an assumed name or make Julie swipe my card through the register every time she goes shopping.

But what kind of an example would that set for my children?

Then I had an idea.

"What are you doing with the scissors?" my husband asked.

"I'm getting our privacy back," I said as I cut through the card. "Then I'm going to the store to buy some TV dinners and processed cheese food—at full price!" I tossed the pieces over my shoulder and let out a crazy little laugh.

"Say, have you been in the cooking sherry again?"

I shook my head and wistfully recalled the good old days before electronic club cards when I had to cut coupons out of the newspaper by hand and could buy a dozen boxes of macaroni and cheese without it going on my permanent record.

I was so happy and innocent then.

Speed Reading

This may surprise and shock you, but the other day as I was barreling down the freeway at exactly the legal speed limit, I passed a motorist who had a book on his lap and was reading as if he were in the study section of the local library.

Of course, as a parent and teacher, I've always been a big advocate of literacy in any type of circumstance, but somehow this just felt wrong.

Maybe it's because I'm the type of person who will be driving along happily in a straight line, then glance down to change the radio station and practically end up in another lane three states over.

Or perhaps it's because the driver was managing to get through a whole chapter without being distracted by children in the backseat shouting, "She's breathing my air!" while they threw plastic fast food toys out the window.

Or maybe it's because I can't believe that all these years I've been busy in the car doing things like keeping my eyes on the road, while I could've been catching up on my reading. As much as I drive, I could've been through *War and Peace* plus all forty-five books of Dana Fuller Ross's *Wagons West* series by now.

Now don't get me wrong. I don't advocate reading while driving, of course. But if someone can drive 65 miles an hour and concentrate on a book, why can't I do something mindless like, say, ironing? Or sorting laundry? In fact, now that I've seen that driving is possible without actually watching traffic, I can get all sorts of housework done on the road. Maybe even balance the checkbook or catch up on putting pictures in the kids' photo albums. And in real heavy traffic, I could make the armrest into a little cutting board, chop fresh vegetables, and have a whole salad ready by the time I arrive home from the mall.

Oh I know that getting behind the wheel can evoke extreme, bizarre behavior in otherwise sane people, but I must say, this is the first time I've ever seen driving turn someone into a book-worm.

Take my friend Sandy, a soft-spoken, reserved woman, who volunteers her time at the local school and gives money to charity. However, once behind the wheel she shouts, "Hey Doofus, quit picking your nose and hit the gas!" to any vehicle in front of her not taking off like a dragster the very second a light turns green.

Now, this I can understand.

And it's not only Sandy. Behind the wheel I'm no longer a petite, almost middle-aged, mother-of-two. I am a powerful Honda—with good gas mileage and an overwhelming urge to be first. I'm not sure why I feel this way. Normally I'm not a competitive person—I don't even like sports. It must have something to do with a primitive fear that if I let enough cars get in front of me, I will eventually end up back where I started.

Oh, deep down I know that this is physically impossible. But so (I'd thought) was reading while driving.

I mean, I see where it could be entertaining and a big time saver and all that, but on top of the obvious dangers, I just can't imagine explaining to a police officer that I forgot to stop at the red light because I was just getting to the chapter where the detective announces who committed the murder; or telling my insurance agent that the accident wasn't my fault, it was really the fault of, say, Danielle Steele.

So even though I might be crazy to pass up the opportunity to better utilize my time, for now I'll stick to driving the old fashioned way—with both eyes on the road.

The Other Woman

My four-year-old son Ben has thrown me over for another woman.

Oh, it all began innocently enough. I'd pick him up from preschool and he'd tell me all about his day finger-painting or coloring. My first inkling that something was amiss came when he started mentioning circle time with a faraway look in his eyes.

"Did you know Miss Linda sang us a song about a pizza?" he'd say wistfully.

At first I didn't mind. I was pleased that he liked his teacher and had adapted so well to his new school. But after a few weeks, his good-bye kisses turned into a quick hug before he bolted out of my arms towards the building block area. A week later he just casually waved good-bye from the Play-Doh table across the room. I expected him to eventually stop me at the door, shake my hand and say, "Well, I'll see you 'round sometime."

I began to worry when I noticed other signs of his infatuation. Like the time he asked me why my glasses weren't round like Miss Linda's. Or why I didn't double knot his tennis shoes. Or the time he insisted that I wasn't writing his name correctly on his lunch bag because, "Miss Linda doesn't make 'Bs' like that."

It was obvious that I was no longer on the top of the "A" list. My popularity had slid farther down the alphabet, landing somewhere behind yams and zucchini.

When I enrolled Ben in preschool, I never expected something like this to happen. I wanted him to learn to write his name, have a good time and make new friends. I had no idea that when I dropped him off each day to learn the alphabet and sort blocks that he was also acquiring independence. Or that by the end of the winter, Miss Linda would rise to movie star status while I became nothing more than another pair of outstretched hands—good only for wiping noses and serving peanut butter and jelly sandwiches.

Now this came as quite a shock since only a few short months ago, I was The Smartest and Most Favorite Person in the Universe! Life was so simple then.

I'd spend my days showing him how to ride a two-wheeled bike without the training wheels or holding his hand when he insisted on wobbling around the block in his new pair of roller-skates. Sometimes we'd bake cookies or take a picnic to the park. And back then, if I had to leave him at a babysitter to run errands he'd cry, "Mommy," and rush into my arms when I returned.

But all that's over now.

Sometimes I wonder what Miss Linda has that I haven't got. After all, Miss Linda is middle-aged, bespectacled, and the mother of four grown children. When I ask my son about it he just sighs and says, "Miss Linda has tadpoles."

But I have a feeling it could also be her big flashy apron with the bunny rabbit pockets, or the way she always has fresh ground coffee beans ready in the sand table for digging, or dozens of Ziploc Baggies filled with homemade purple Play-Doh, or the fact that she sings animal songs with all of the correct finger movements. Or maybe, just maybe, it's because she showed him how to finger-paint with ice cubes for the very first time.

In the beginning I tried to ignore his new infatuation. I tried not to mind the hurried good-byes or his obvious preference for spending a day at preschool rather than at home with me. But it didn't work. After a while I only felt worse—because he didn't seem to mind, either.

Then I considered having a heart-to-heart talk with Miss Linda. I pictured sitting down like a mature adult and congratulating her on the wonderful way she has with children. I would praise her creative ingenuity, then grab her by the apron strings and demand to know just what she thought she was doing manipulating my son's affection with homemade Play-Doh. And I'd tell her in no uncertain terms that she wasn't the only one around here who could say the Pledge of Allegiance in sign language and make cricket sounds by rubbing both hands together. But I had a feeling she wouldn't understand.

So I did the only thing a secure and sensible mother could do: I used my wiles to try to lure my son back.

Unfortunately, I began by reading him a bedtime story that he'd already heard in preschool. He sat on my lap as I read and stopped me halfway through the first page.

"Miss Linda lets us see the pictures first," he said.

I turned the book towards him and continued reading up-side down.

"And Mom," he said, "you forgot to make the animal sounds."

I pointed at the pictures and did my best. But unfortunately, where I barked Miss Linda had "whoofed;" where I neighed, she had whinnied; and where I oinked, she had definitely snorted.

"You're not doing it right," my son said, exasperated. "Maybe I should just go to sleep."

"No! Not yet," I protested.

We somehow got through the rest of the story but when I gave him a kiss and turned out the light, I thought I heard him sigh.

The next night I decided to show my son just how fun and hip I could be, so I suggested we skip the story and sing silly songs instead. This was my chance to shine; after all, I'd been singing since my oldest child was born eight years ago. But halfway through the "Itsy Bitsy Spider," my son informed me that not only was I singing different words than Miss Linda; I wasn't making the spider correctly with my fingers.

And, on top of that, when I tried to cut his apple in the special way Miss Linda did so he could see the star inside, he claimed he couldn't see it.

Things were so much easier when I was popular.

One afternoon, however, just when I was ready to pack up and go live with a family that liked me, my son grabbed my hand and said, "Mommy, will you play with me?" And we sat on the living room floor and built the tallest block skyscraper ever and then demolished it. We baked cookies and ate the raw batter off the spoon. Then we went to the park and dug moats in the wet sand with plastic shovels—just like the good old days.

And for a brief time, I basked in the sunlight of being number one again.

Of course I knew it wouldn't last, but I've come to accept my fleeting popularity because deep down I know that there are some things that Miss Linda can't do: like go to all of Ben's soccer games and cheer the loudest every time he makes a goal, or celebrate the first time he rides a two-wheeled bike without training wheels, or give him a kiss after tucking him into bed for the night.

Oh, a part of me still wants to grab Miss Linda by the apron strings and demand my son back, but another part realizes that I haven't lost my place on the "A" list, I've just been rotated to another spot for a while. And since I have an older child, I know that when the novelty of ice-painting and purple Play-Doh wears off, I will once again reclaim my place as the Smartest Most Favorite Person in the Universe.

At least until my son starts kindergarten.

Mark My Words
(AND THE FURNITURE AND THE WALLS...)

$\mathcal{M}$om Advice

Shocking as this may seem, the other day—in the middle of the afternoon—a fantasy of mine came true. Oh, I don't mean the passionate running-away-to-live-with-Fabio-in-a-cottage-by-the-sea type fantasy. Although there's nothing wrong with that, mind you. But I'm talking about the other kind: revenge. I mean, there I was at the park leisurely watching my children climbing up the slide and eating sand, and here comes a young mother with a new baby dozing in the stroller. A new baby!

And let me just say that as a mother of a five- and eight-year-old, there's nothing I like more in the world than finding someone who knows less about raising children than I do.

Call me strange, but I couldn't wait to walk right up to her and start saying things like, "I think the baby is hungry" or "What do you mean she's not eating bowls of cereal yet?" And, "Why isn't the baby wearing a hat? It's still mid April, you know."

Of course, I wasn't always this way. But there's something about being the recipient of several years worth of unsolicited advice that somehow changes you in inexplicable, mysterious ways.

Face it, when you venture out of the house with a baby, people who normally wouldn't dare speak to you can't wait to point out ways you can improve yourself as a parent. It's as if they instinctively know you can't program the VCR or balance the checkbook, so therefore, can't be trusted to take care of a child all by yourself.

And let me just say that no place is safe. Once you have a child, no matter where you go, little old ladies will come flying out of the woodwork to give you pointers on all sorts of things, like how to cure gas and avoid constipation. Like the time my three-year-old daughter had a tantrum in the grocery store because I wouldn't let her out of the cart so she could pick out all of the food herself.

"Why don't you just give her what she wants?" said a sweet, little old lady standing behind us.

Much to my credit, I didn't yell. I mean, you can't just go around raising your voice to sweet little old ladies. Instead, I smiled politely and wondered what she would say if she knew that what my daughter really wanted was a chance to hurl all the canned corn off shelves, squeeze the bananas, eat a blue Popsicle from the freezer section, and catapult her Gymnastic Barbie from the seat of the cart into the produce scale.

I must admit, a part of me was tempted to throw my arms out to my sides and say, "You know, you're absolutely right!" Then whip out adoption papers from my purse and transfer my daughter into her cart. But I'm not that mean.

Then there was the time I ventured to the mall with my five-month-old son and was stopped by a complete stranger. "That baby is bored," she announced. "He needs something to play with." So, like a good mother, I took out his educational activity wheel from the diaper bag and put it on the tray in the stroller. Then five minutes later, I was stopped by a different woman who announced that my baby was being "over stimulated," so I tossed the wheel back into my purse and took out a frozen teething rattle. I thought that would be the end of it until yet another woman approached, shook her finger accusingly at me, and said, "He'll poke his eye out with that thing and *then* you'll be sorry."

So now you probably understand why I could hardly contain myself when I saw a mother with a new baby at the park. Let's face it, I couldn't wait to set her straight by telling her all about the danger of hatless babies, the magic effect of clothes dryers on colic, places to store extra binkies, my conclusion to the cloth versus disposable debate, and how to wind up a swing without waking the baby.

But truth be told, when I looked down at the baby, all that came out of my mouth was, "Gee, what beautiful blue eyes he has."

Granted, it wasn't a very helpful or especially insightful thing to say, but some day she'll thank me for it.

$\mathcal{S}$elf Talk

Okay, I admit it. I'm one of those people addicted to self-help books. I can tell you how to get the truth in five minutes or less in any conversation. I've wandered the spiritual path to higher creativity. And I can state the Nine Fantasies that will ruin your life along with the eight realties that will save it.

On top of that, I've posed in the lotus position longer than most Buddhists, I've studied the Art of Zen, and I can say *Om Namo Narayanayayanaya* ten times in a row without stopping.

By now some of you are probably thinking that with all this information, I should be a fairly enlightened person. You would think.

So you can imagine my surprise when I heard about a new method for personal improvement called "self talk." This simply means that you can feel calm or worried or even change your behavior depending on what you tell yourself.

Let me stop right here and say that this is exactly the type of thing that makes this decade so refreshing. I mean, if at any other time in history you told people that you were listening to voices in your head, they might make all kinds of unflattering assumptions. But now it's not only acceptable to listen to them, they're *supposed* to be there. You can't imagine what a relief this is.

Naturally there are some ground rules, though. For example, you're supposed to say positive, uplifting things to yourself like, "Gee, I feel a little stressed, but I'm going to find a way healthy way to relax," other than, "Don't you even *think* about eating that piece of cake. Keep it up, and pretty soon you'll be trading in your lucky jeans for a set of gingham muumuus."

Another important rule (even with scientific progress being what it is today) is that it's best to talk internally rather than carrying on heated conversations with yourself in places like, say, department store dressing rooms.

However, despite these restrictions, I am perfectly willing to try this. In fact, you will hardly find anyone else on the planet more willing to talk to him or herself than I am. Besides (and this may come as a shock), I am a person with many unresolved issues—most of which revolve around some form of shopping.

So the very next time I was in one of those big warehouse stores, I decided to use self-talk to control my spending habits.

Just look at that, I thought as I wandered down the personal necessity aisle, *a bag of eight hairbrushes for only ten dollars! What a deal!*

Come on, my logical inner voice piped up. *What in the heck are you going to do with all those brushes?*

Well, I can give them as gifts or use the larger ones as door stops.

You don't need them, it said firmly.

Oh, but I do! I do! The orange one alone would cost me $7.50 at the beauty parlor, I pleaded.

"Remember the time you bought a pack of thirty-two golf balls and ended up using them to border the flowerbed?"

"But . . ."

"Put them back. NOW!"

"Make me!"

I could tell by the way people were backing away from me that I had started speaking out loud. So I quickly returned the brushes to the shelf and grabbed a bottle of hairspray instead.

As soon as I left the aisle, I felt proud of my new self-control. But then I arrived in the bakery section and my inner self proceeded to talk me out of buying four dozen dinner rolls.

And if that wasn't enough, when I went to the deli department for a gallon of potato salad my inner voice talked me out of that, too.

The final straw came when I reached for a twenty-five pound box of laundry detergent.

"But you can't possibly use all tha . . ."

"*Shut up*," I said, tossing the box into the cart.

Needless to say, I did save money and although there was nothing edible in the house, I felt good about it. In fact, when the men with straight jackets show up at my door to take me away to a nice padded room, I'll just explain all about self-talk and feeling empowered and changing behavior and all that.

On second thought, maybe I'd better just say *Om Namo Narayanayayanaya.*

The Third Time's a Charm

I've never been one to hold much stock in lucky numbers. Lately, however, the number three has taken on a magical quality at my house. Now by magical, I don't mean disappearing elephants or flying carpets or anything like that. But it seems that no one, *no one* in my family can hear anything I say until after I've said it at least three times.

Now normally I've always considered three a lucky number. After all, it's the amount of wishes you get from a Genie, the number of chances you get before you strike out, the number of kittens who lost their mittens, and so on. But let's face it, after you become a parent, three somehow loses its appeal.

For example, every morning about five minutes before the carpool arrives to pick up my children for school, I say in my best patient Mommy voice, "You'd better move along now, the carpool will be here any minute." To which my children respond by ignoring me completely or jumping to their feet and rushing into the living room to turn on the television.

Now like most parents, I'm a bit less patient the second time around. So I say something like, "Hurry up for gosh sakes! You're going to be late!" This time my stern tone and no-nonsense attitude causes my daughter to run into the living room and play every song she knows on the piano.

Needless to say, by the third time I have to repeat myself my eyes are bulging out of their sockets, my face is purple from lack of oxygen, and I'm desperately shouting all sorts of phrases straight from the glossary of the Joan Crawford parenting manual—to which my children respond by rolling their eyes and saying, "Geez, Mom, we can hear you. You don't have to yell at us, you know."

Now don't get me wrong, it's not like I don't know what to do. I mean, I've read books on how to talk so kids will listen, how to listen so kids will talk, how to inject kids with self-esteem, how to deflate inflated egos, how to parent the strong-willed child and all that. Believe me, I've read them all. So you would think I'd be able to make two children listen to instructions the first time I say them. You would think.

It's not like I haven't tried. One time I decided to repeat each request three times real fast, just to get it over with. For weeks I went through my day saying things like, "Wash your hands, wash your hands, wash your hands," until strangers began backing away from me in public places.

Frankly, I could've lived with this, but the problem was that my children sensed it was a trick. I'm not sure why, but my theory is that each statement must be evenly spaced ten minutes apart or it will only be considered as one long first request, which every parent knows is nothing but a big waste of time because no one will hear you anyway.

I must admit though, we did have a big breakthrough the other day.

I was talking on the phone to my friend Julie and spelled out "c-a-n-d-y" in a whisper during our conversation. Both of my children instantly dropped what they were doing, fell to their knees, and hung onto my every word as if I was some kind of new age, modern day prophet.

And guess what, the same thing happened when I said the words "ice cream cone," "chocolate bar," and "fast food."

So clearly, all you need to do to be heard by your children is work one of these seven key words into every sentence.

But then, of course, it couldn't hurt to say it two more times anyway—just for good measure.

The Best Laid Plans

I used to be a perfect parent. I had strong opinions about the best way to raise a happy, healthy, well-mannered child. I vowed that my children would appear well groomed and clean at all times. They would be disciplined by firm, fair and consistent parenting techniques and they would always, *always*, be well behaved in a restaurant. And when they were older, I would instill a sense of self-confidence and mutual respect by showing them that I valued their opinions and by treating them as equals. My ideas were so straightforward and simple that I couldn't understand why other parents couldn't be as perfect as I was.

Then I had children.

I used to think that any mother whose child was inappropriately dressed and had Kool Aid stains around his lips before eleven o'clock in the morning, was obviously an unfit parent who spent the day talking on the phone, and who served Fruit Loops and popsicles for breakfast.

My opinion changed when my daughter turned two and decided that she no longer wanted to wear clothing in public. One minute she would be fully dressed, innocently sucking on a pacifier in her stroller. And the next, she'd be waving at strangers wearing only a diaper and a pair of red patent leather shoes. The first few times this happened I kept putting her clothes back on—only to have them flung at me again two seconds later. After several days of struggling to keep her fully dressed, I finally decided that it would be less stressful and much faster if she just started out naked when we left the house.

I also used to think that parents who let their children watch cartoons instead of doing enriching activities together, like reading, lacked self-discipline and motivation. This was before I began daydreaming about how great it would be if my four-year-old son stopped making big messes around the house and did nothing but watch TV. There would be no toys to pick up, no Play-Doh to peel out of the carpet and no crayons to remove from nostrils. Besides, I figured if he got really hooked on a few afternoon cartoons, I might even have time to do things like put on a real pair of shoes with laces—or finish a complete thought without being interrupted.

Before I had children I was going to be a good, health-conscious parent. My family would only eat organic produce and dairy products, fresh fruit, yeast-free bread, and un-medicated free-range turkey. Sugar would never, ever touch their lips.

I changed my mind when I brought my daughter to the grocery store for the first time by myself, and she refused to bend her legs so she could fit into the front seat of the shopping cart. "If you get in the cart, Mommy will give you part of the nice candy bar she has in her purse," I whispered desperately in her ear.

This tactic worked well until she had eaten all of the candy. Then she decided the trip would be much more interesting if she got out of the cart and flung all of the food off the shelves as she ran down the aisles. So I did what any other modern, educated mother would do: I desperately started tossing junk food into the cart. She ate the box of mini donuts in the dairy aisle, munched on fistfuls of caramel corn in the produce section, and the Tootsie Pop sucker gave me just enough time to get through the register, out the door and back to my car.

It occurred to me, as I loaded bags full of empty boxes and wrappers into my trunk, that the only obstacle keeping me from being a perfect parent—was my children.

Like the time I vowed that my son would never play with weapons. But even though I felt that only irresponsible parents let their children play with toy guns, it didn't seem to stop my son from turning just about everything into one. One day my son made a gun out of a banana and shot the cat as he was eating lunch. I was worried when I saw the gleam in his eyes as he shouted, "Bang!" and his obvious disappointment when the cat didn't stop what it was doing, clutch its chest, and fall down on the floor.

And how was I supposed to know when I vowed to never lie to my children that my five-year-old daughter would begin asking me questions about the reproductive process long before I was ready to tell her?

I finally compromised by discussing a few key facts, using the animal kingdom as an example. I thought I handled the subject honestly and tactfully—until she began to approach everyone that came to our home and say, "Do you have a uterus?" as if it were a pick-up line in a seedy bar. Then, if they unwittingly answered yes, she'd demand to know what size it was, where it came from, and if she could take a look at it.

Now when my children go into public, I want to stop people and let them know that I am really a good parent. I want to tell them that my son is eating a Popsicle for breakfast because he's going through a phase where he will only eat blue food and I'm running out of options. He has a dirty dishtowel tucked into the back of his shirt because he thinks it's a cape and today he wants to be Batman. And my daughter is wearing her bathing suit with a pair of cowboy boots because she picked out her own outfit and she thinks the leather tassels go great with the pink netting on her skirt.

And when I yell things like, "Because I'm the Mommy and I said so, that's why!" I really mean, "I can understand your desire, but it is my duty as a concerned mother to constantly look out for your best interests."

Sometimes I wonder how it would feel to appear in public with two orderly, quiet children with immaculate faces and clean clothes. I could shop without anyone repeating, "Can I have a big pretzel now Mommy?" every three seconds like some sort of hypnotic mantra. Maybe I could even stop to look at something. Or enter a store, get only what I actually need, then leave!

But I have a feeling my life wouldn't be nearly as exciting.

And now, when I see a mother with a child who is happily meandering behind her eating a Twinkie and wearing wrinkled dinosaur pajamas and a pair of swim fins, I no longer think she's an unfit parent—I know she's just doing the best she can.

How Embarrassing!

I often wonder why, out of all the parenting books I read during my pregnancy, not one ever mentioned the Embarrassment Factor. I learned a great deal about handling colic, what to expect during various developmental stages and how to deal with temper tantrums, but nobody properly prepared me for hanging out with an unreasonable human being whose embarrassing behavior made me want to crawl under a rock every time I left the house.

I knew there were some things about parenting that I couldn't control when my daughter started blurting out personal information like a miniature public address system everywhere we went. By the time we'd leave a store, I felt like every person there knew my name, where I went to college, my real weight (including shoes), how I voted in the last election, and my feelings on the depletion of the ozone layer and what exactly I intended to do about it. And that was only if I needed to buy a few things. But back then I thought it would pass in time. Little did I know that the Embarrassment Factor strikes early and only increases with age.

Like when my daughter turned four and insisted on dressing herself. I'd lay out two different colored dresses with patent leather shoes on the end of her bed to choose from. But she had a different idea. Each morning she'd emerge from her room wearing a pair of rain boots, a bike helmet, and the dirtiest pair of jeans she could find from the hamper. She didn't dress up like a fairy princess or ballerina like I remember doing as a child. She was a superhero.

At first I tried all of the usual things: like giving her restrictive choices, hiding all of the super hero accessories, and trying to dress her while she was still asleep. When these didn't work, I considered making a button to pin on her cape that said, *"This outfit does not reflect the opinion of management."*

As time went on, she began taking her superhero role more seriously by sporadically blurting out select crime-fighting phrases in public. One day we were standing in line in the grocery store and a nice elderly woman behind us made the mistake of making eye contact with her.

"What a beautiful little girl," she said. "Is that your Halloween costume?"

My daughter looked at her for a moment, then put up two hands karate-style and shouted, "Back off clay brain! It's morphing time!"

After that I decided it would be easier to walk several feet ahead or behind her—just enough to keep her in sight without anyone knowing we were together.

Then one day she decided she wanted more information about the reproductive process—preferably in a crowded public place.

"Mommy, where did I come from?" she'd ask while I unloaded the groceries in line at the checkout stand.

"My tummy." I was proud of my honest response.

"How did I get there?"

It seemed as if everybody within twenty feet stopped what they were doing and waited for my reply as I frantically tried to think of an appropriate public, and biologically correct, answer.

"The stork," I finally whispered.

She pondered this as I finished unloading the cart.

"Nuh-uh!" she said finally. Then she gave up and turned to the lady standing behind us. "Do you have a UTERUS?"

Luckily for our friends and neighbors, she eventually outgrew her fascination with the reproductive process. In our naïveté, we also thought she had matured, so we took her out to dinner to an upscale restaurant that had full-size chairs and complete sets of metal silverware.

My daughter must've been in shock since the first fifteen minutes went extraordinarily well. None of the other customers scooted their tables to the other side of the room, or requested we leave. Then the meal arrived.

My daughter looked at her spaghetti and cried, "Look, snakes!"

"No wait!" she cried. "It's a pile of worms! Hahahahaha!"

I cringed as the people at the other tables began to stare at my dysfunctional family.

"Wait," she cried, "it's guts!" She slapped her hand down on the table and burst into hysterics. "Bloody worm guts! Hahahahahahaha!"

"Shhhhh!" I hissed. "This is not how to behave in a restaurant."

She considered this for a moment, then looked down at her plate and burst into laughter again. In fact, she seemed so impressed with her own jokes that I half expected her to pack up the food and complimentary crayons and hit the late night talk show circuit—I bet most of the people in the room wished she had.

Afterwards, my friends assured me this was normal behavior; but I secretly blamed the diet soda I drank in the final trimester of my pregnancy. Then my friend Jenny told me her six-year-old daughter snuck one of her good negligees to school for sharing and lost it somewhere on the playground during recess. But I think she was just trying to make me feel better.

The real turning point came several weeks later when my daughter had a friend over to play Barbies. Her friend picked up a doll and casually announced, "My Mommy can't wear a bathing suit because she has cream cheese on the back of her legs."

Then it occurred to me that no matter how bad things seem, they could always be worse.

Now that my daughter is eight years old, I know that being embarrassed is a normal part of being a parent. And that's okay, because I know I'll get my chance to embarrass her—just as soon as she becomes a teenager.

℘arent Speak

People warned me that once I had children things would change. They told me all about sleepless nights and endless diaper changes. They also filled me in on pacifiers, the difference between teething and ear infections, and how nothing in my life, or on my body, would ever be the same again. But no one dared to tell me the whole truth of it: that having children would affect my vocabulary.

Back in college I used to be able to discuss important world issues in both a coherent and sophisticated manner. But now, after eight years of raising two children, I hear myself saying things like, "You come now here."

And it's not just me.

One day when we were visiting my relatives, my sister-in-law Donna, an intelligent person who has a master's degree in psychology, called out to her children, "Eat now stop play you!" and I understood exactly what she meant.

But what's funny is how automatic this new way of speaking is. One day it seems you're an articulate, childless person with a corner office and a window, and the next day you find yourself in a park surrounded by children, muttering things that no one has ever heard spoken before in the English language.

In fact, my last conversation with a childless person was right after I'd stayed up all night with a teething toddler. It went something like this:

Her: Do you think the change of political party in the White House will affect the balance of the national economy, and possibly wipe out social security as we know it?

Me: Nah.

Her: And don't you agree that what the government needs to do is put regulations on risky investments to prevent the inevitable turn of the stock market from wiping out millions of short term investors?

Me: Yeyawh, fop nitty noop.

Suddenly I was met with the kind of stare usually reserved for naked people running through the street. But let's face it, what I really meant to say was, "Exactly, as long as restrictions don't cause upheaval in the world market and upset the balance of the national economy." And I'm sure I don't have to tell you that if she were a parent, she would've known this.

Of course, I occasionally have good moments when I have the mental energy to string two complete thoughts together into a whole sentence and I feel positively glib. But those moments never last and I inevitably fall back into my old inarticulate ways.

So you can't blame me for seeking out people who I can relate to. In fact, the other day I was startled when a well-dressed woman standing in front of me at the grocery store said to the clerk, "How much is that blue thingy-ma-bob hanging next to the wood what-cha-ma-call-it?" And I immediately felt at ease because I knew I was in the company of a fellow mother.

Oh, I know that having such a limited vocabulary has some drawbacks, but it can be quite useful. For instance, since you no longer need to worry about irrelevant things like the English language, you'll have more energy for getting your toddler dressed and shoveling out your good silverware from the bottom of the sandbox. Plus few people can argue with you, mainly because no one can figure out what you're talking about.

But I must admit, deep down I'm worried about the kind of example I'm setting for my children. After all, I want them to grow up to be articulate, successful adults.

Then the other day my almost nine-year-old daughter put her arms around me and said, "Ta for the jiggy necklace, Mom. You're way phat." She kissed me on the cheek and headed for her room. "Peace out."

All I could say was thanks. But I tried to say it nicely.

$\mathcal{M}$y Daughter, My Self

Many years ago, in the midst of my rebellious teenage years, my mother used to say, "Just wait until you have a daughter of your own. I hope she's just like you!"

I always suspected that this was a form of revenge rather than a compliment. But now that I'm a mother, it's apparent that the age-old, maternal curse has backfired: instead of having a daughter just like me, I have a daughter who's just like my mother.

In fact, they get along so well that I've begun to suspect that I'm really living with a sixty-something woman stuffed into the body of a third grader. As impossible as this may sound, it would sure explain a lot of things. Like why, for instance, when my daughter was five years old her favorite dress up outfit was a mid-length polyester dress with a wide lace collar, a pair of white gloves, patent leather shoes, and a red, clasp handbag. While I spent my kindergarten years dressed up like a ballerina or fairy princes, flitting around casting spells and all sorts of magical things, my daughter spent hers looking more like Queen Elizabeth leaving the Royal Palace for a luncheon. Strangely enough, my mother has the same outfit. You can't just ignore a coincidence like that.

Oh, of course I love my daughter and I'm happy she idolizes her grandmother and all that, but I can't help wondering how I'm supposed to relate to such a puzzling child who's so different from me.

I mean, how in the world can I ever understand a daughter who likes to embroider pillowcases? Like I've told you, I'm the type of person whose sewing kit contains a bunch of dull pins, some dental floss, and a stapler. I acquired my only domestic training in the home economics class I was forced to take in high school because the art classes were full. You'll remember how I spent the entire semester trying to thread the sewing machine, and only succeeded in stitching a seam up my right arm, forcing me to pull the cord out of the wall with my foot. So you can imagine how having a daughter who knows the difference between a backstitch and a French knot would baffle someone like me.

Sometimes I wonder if I'm doing something wrong. But it's not like I'm not trying. One time, when she wanted to bake home-made cookies, I bought a bucket of cookie dough and cleaned out all of the extra wrapping paper and shoeboxes that I usually stored in the oven. But I don't think she was fooled by my feeble attempt at domesticity.

Many years ago I used to imagine having a daughter just like me. I pictured us having a great time cooking frozen pizza together, scattering shoes around and stapling up the hems of our pants. We'd go hiking together and stay up late watching old movies— and we'd have no idea what a satin stitch is. But instead, I have a mysterious daughter whose personality traits have somehow skipped a generation.

However, I noticed something strange the day she wanted me to help her sew a new dress.

"How about tie dying a tee-shirt in the bathtub instead?" I suggested hopefully.

"No way!" she said, rolling her eyes. And I was shocked to see the same eye roll I used to give my own mother many years ago.

After that I began to notice other things as well. Like how we both laugh at the same corny jokes and have trouble doing long division. Or how we hum when we're nervous or don't like to wear socks with our tennis shoes and how we love butterflies.

The real proof came the day she decided she wanted to roller skate because she saw the other children in the neighborhood doing it. She went onto the driveway and strapped her skates and helmet on. Then she refused to let anyone help her, even though she kept falling down over and over again. But by dinnertime she had taught herself how to skate like the others.

Underneath the surface, my daughter and I are more alike than I thought. Oh, of course, now that she's entering her rebellious teenage years, she's used the old eye-roll plenty of times. And when that happens, I want to tell her in my best "I've been there" kind of voice, that all of the rules are for her own good. And that I love her and want her to grow up to be safe and responsible and all that.

But instead, all that comes out is, "Just wait until you have a daughter of your own".

ℳ Long-Standing Date

I have to warn you now. If you're already feeling a little sad and gloomy, I suggest you move right along down the page because, you see, I am sitting here writing this story on a Sunday. Now most of you are probably thinking, "Big deal. What's so gloomy about that?" And you're right. There's really nothing inherently gloomy about it except, of course, that this is the first story I ever wrote on a Sunday.

And it's not because I have anything against writing on Sundays, mind you, it's because for the last 36 years I've always had a long-standing date. A date with a very special man, 56 years older than me.

Oh, before you start doing the addition and notifying the authorities and all that, I want you to know that I'm not talking about anything dangerous or illegal or sordid here. I'm talking about a date with my grandfather.

Let me stop right here and say, no matter what your age, no one can dispute the mysterious bond between grandparents and grandchildren. Maybe it's because grandparents have a reputation of being easy. I mean, it doesn't take much to make them think you're the most wonderfully brilliant person ever born on the face of the planet. And the nice thing is, all you have to do to achieve this status is to, say, breathe. Face it, who can resist someone who thinks you're the Princess of the Entire Universe?

And, on top of that, there are the grandparentish activities.

These are all of the things that our parents wouldn't do with us. Like hanging out at the airport and watching the planes take off on the runway or eating ice cream bars with your fingers on the good sofa before dinner.

When I was young, our Sundays together consisted of a whirlwind of zoos and carnivals, adventurous bus rides and park play structures. During my teenage years we moved on to PG rated movies and eating ice cream at outdoor malls.

As we both grew older, our Sunday dates expanded to include my children. My grandfather couldn't drive anymore so we picked him up and took him for rides in the car. Sometimes we brought him to our house for dinner. Or he played checkers with my kids.

At 92 years of age, he remained astonishingly independent. The only problem was that our phone calls began to sound less like a conversation and more like a bad Abbot and Costello routine.

They went something like, "Grandpa, do you need me to bring you some soup? Bananas? Noodles? "

"What? Did you say I need some poodles?"

"NOODLES," I'd shout into the receiver.

"STRUDELS?" he'd shout back. "What in the heck would I want those for?"

Eventually using the phone became so harrowing that if I needed to tell him something really important, it was safer to drive the 20 miles to his house and tell him in person.

By now you're probably wondering why I'm telling you all this. And truth be told, I probably wouldn't be, except today I saw a mother with two young children and a grandmotherly-looking lady in a local coffee shop, having their own Sunday date.

I admit, a part of me wanted to interrupt them and tell them all about my grandfather. About how Sunday was always our day, too. And how he was born in 1910 and worked in the shipyards during World War II. How he had enjoyed taking cruises and always had the most *joie de vivre* of anyone I knew. And about how, from now on, things will never be the same again.

But I didn't.

Instead I went quickly home to work on this story. Not because I'm in a hurry, you see, but because it's Sunday and my standing dates have come to an end.

And somehow that just makes me cry.

A FEW FOR THE ROAD

Crazy Preschool Quirks

If you ever feel that your life isn't crazy enough, try hanging around with a preschooler for a while. Trust me, reality as you've come to know it will suddenly take a drastic turn for the lunatic fringe.

Sure, it may sound like a gross exaggeration. We all know that preschoolers do a lot of normal things like, say, dress in adorable costumes and laugh at stupid knock-knock jokes. That's part of their charm. However, don't let this act fool you. Most preschoolers have quirks that even Howard Hughes would think are strange.

For example, take my friend Cheryl. Lately she can't get anywhere on time because she has to stand on the driveway waiting for her four-year-old Maddie, an only child, to buckle all of her imaginary friends into the minivan.

"We are now up to six," she said one day over coffee. "There are the two imaginary baby sitters, Gia and Jenny; two imaginary friends, Rayanne and Taylor; the imaginary siblings, Sally (age 1 1/2) and Merky (age 7); and one imaginary rabbit, Munchie." She leaned over and clutched my arm nervously. "If she adds one more imaginary thing I'll have to get a bigger car."

If you think that's bad, there are my friends Lisa and Carol. The first has a four-year-old daughter who has a grudge against any type of clothing with buttons and will only eat rainbow frosting and French fries. The latter has a five-year-old who isn't picky about her wardrobe or what kind of food she eats as long as it's served with a frayed fuchsia plastic spoon with a smiling parrot on the handle, ironically referred to as "The Happy Spoon."

Okay, so this may not sound like such a crisis to you, however it's the only piece left out of the original baby jungle-themed dinner set, thus guaranteeing no replacement if ever lost or destroyed. Which, as most parents know, is only a matter of time. And to suggest using another spoon is simply a laughable idea.

Really, it's amazing that with all these self-imposed rules and regulations preschoolers make any progress at all.

And it's no use reasoning with them. Sure, you can try launching into your ten part lecture series, *You Can't Just Go around Avoiding Buttons and Living on Rainbow Frosting Forever, You Know*, but they'll only stare at you with the same sort of look reserved for major losers and Mr. Roger's reruns. It's then you realize that you have now entered into a battle of wits in which you have no weapons.

And then there's my friend Nadine. She's resigned herself to sitting propped up in the hall outside her eight-year-old triplets' room until they fall asleep. "The worst part is that they've just come to expect it. It used to be that if I tried to sneak off, one of them would look out the door and yell, 'I'm scared!' Now they just look out and say, 'Hey, where'd you go?'"

I admit, hearing stuff like this suddenly makes my children seem more normal. I mean, let's face it, what's carving three dozen sandwiches into the shape of a kitten compared to *that*?

Oh sure, I know what you're thinking. You're thinking that only spineless fools let their children get away with this kind of stuff. And you're right. But I prefer to think of it more as choosing my own battles.

And that's exactly why I just helped my son pick out all of the orange fruit loops from the cereal box so he can carry them around the house in an old tennis shoe.

Me? I'm saving my strength for the teenage years.

Developing Pictures

I don't want to brag, but I've always thought of myself as, well, a fairly educated person. I know how to set a thermostat, program a VCR and work a computer by myself. I can, for the most part, balance a checkbook, pump my own gas and make a mean eggplant casserole.

But no matter how hard I try, I can't figure out the local drug store's system for processing film.

Okay, okay. Some of you more savvy types are probably thinking, "What's the big deal, Lady? You go to the counter, fill out the envelope, slip it into the slot and voilà! A spider monkey could do it."

Others of you (and you know who you are) know *exactly* what I mean. You're the kind of person who charges into the photo section with gobs of finished rolls of film, pulls out an envelope and then immediately faints dead away on the floor. Suddenly you, a person who graduated Suma cum laude, can't figure out which box to mark. Or what kind of film you have. Or why you're wearing blue sandals with a red skirt. Or where you stand on the whole Harrison Ford dating Calista Flockhart issue. In fact, you're no longer sure of anything anymore.

And don't bother asking me why this happens because, well, I don't know. But I have a feeling it has something to do with all of the choices. I admit, whenever I'm given anything more than three choices, my whole system shuts down.

Like, the other day when I went to drop off my film at the local drugstore, I was immediately surrounded by approximately thirty-two tiny yellow signs, all with various, reasonable sounding, options. Do I want one-day service or two? Double prints or CD disk? Advantage or Advanced film process? How about twelve single 5x7's? Or twenty-four 3x5 triple prints? Color or black and white? And on and on.

There was a weary-looking lady next to me surrounded by a pile of envelopes, each with almost everything crossed out. I immediately relaxed because I knew I was in the company of another hopelessly confused person.

"I can't believe this is so hard," she said turning to me. "Just when I finally got the hang of buying panty hose."

I was in complete sympathy.

In fact, I thought back to the good old days when getting film developed meant putting your 110 cartridge into an envelope with your name scrawled on it. But clearly, this was no longer something to be taken so lightly. Now days, if you make one wrong mark you could end up with something very, very bad. Like the time my friend Julie thought she'd marked single 5x7 prints and she came home with fifty-seven dollars worth of color slides. And she doesn't even own a slide projector.

I admit it's times like this that I envy my friend Shirley, who's gone digital. The only problem is that she has everything from the birth of her son to his seventh birthday party stuck inside of her camera. At last count, she has approximately 7000 pictures in there. But, hey, at least she knows where she stands.

But getting back to my point. After much discussion of size and processing and all that, we decided three important things: 1) you should not, under any circumstances, just mark everything on the envelope and see what happens, 2) Harrison Ford dating Calista Flockhart is just plain wrong, and 3) the best thing to do is choose the section with the 3x5 double prints in color.

We marked our envelopes and slid them through the slot. Then we stood around for a moment and swapped picture developing horror stories before going our separate ways.

And I'd like to tell you that everything turned out okay, but it didn't. Oh sure, I got what I ordered, but when I picked up my film I had 24 double prints of several tiny blurry images that could've either been my family or squirrels, and one particularly colorful picture of my thumb.

And folks, I didn't even scream.

⊛ne Thing Leads to Another

I finally know what is preventing mothers from completing their children's scrapbooks: scotch tape.

I'm not sure why this is—but trust me. The next time you have a whole day to catch up on your scrapbook, you'll be sitting at a table innocently arranging photos on an acid-free background and you'll suddenly think to yourself, "I need the scotch tape." So you get up and wander into the kitchen trying to remember where you last saw it. First you try the catchall drawer, but instead of scotch tape you find three pennies and the missing button from your lucky shirt—which, by the way, would be perfect to wear to the Bunko Game tomorrow night. So you try to find the sewing kit that you remember seeing a couple of months ago "somewhere in the garage"—possibly near the scotch tape dispenser.

However, you must clear a path to get past the furnace because the garage lacks any sort of organization. Luckily you have some spare time, and you're just the person to whip it into shape. So you spend the rest of the morning sifting through boxes of old maternity clothes and power tools. Then, as you're trying to find a place for the wooden table with antler legs your husband made in high school shop class, you decide that things would go a lot smoother if you could just take his treasures to a place where they would be appreciated like, say, a nice charity organization. And you must take them today. In fact, this very minute.

But just as soon as the car is loaded and you pull down the driveway, you notice that the car needs gas, and the only station where you know how to work the pumps for sure is five miles in the opposite direction.

While you're there you decide to get the free car wash which, after all, you've earned by filling up the tank, and you take your place (fifth) in line to wait your turn.

By the time you finish, all the water in the car wash has made you thirsty, so you stop off at a fast food place to get a drink. While you are ordering, you realize you have nothing for dinner, so you go to the grocery store to buy a chicken. Then you decide to add a container of potato salad, a head of lettuce, and a box of cereal for tomorrow's breakfast.

Before you know it, you've finished next week's shopping and are struggling to fit all of the groceries into the trunk between the wooden antlers.

You finally arrive at the donation station two hours after you left the house. While you're unloading the car you have a nice conversation with the attendant about the great weather you've been having, why "no one makes good wood furniture anymore," and the latest episode of ER.

Then you look at your watch and mumble something about having to go because your children will be home any minute. As you get into the car you wonder how the day could go by so fast.

But if you hurry, you might just have enough time to get another picture down in your scrapbook—unless, of course, you remember about the scotch tape.

Mini Vacations

Let's face it; becoming a parent radically alters your vacation plans. Oh, it's not that you lose your desire to travel or anything like that. It's more that your definition of rest and relaxation changes. Instead of jetting off to San Carlo or cruising the Caribbean, you are more than perfectly happy to spend five minutes just about anywhere—alone. But that's not all that changes. Instead of getting an annual two-week vacation at one time, you now have to divide it up into several forty-five minute increments throughout the year. My friend Laura fondly refers to them as "sanity breaks," but I prefer to think of them more as mini vacations.

Personally, one of my favorite destination spots is the local grocery store. In fact, if I drive under the speed limit and miss all the green lights, I can stretch my outing into two, possibly three, hours. Oh, it's not that I don't miss my family back home, but the minute I enter the store and head toward the deli counter for a mocha cappuccino, I develop a whole new personality. I am no longer a suburban mother of two: I am a sightseer on vacation.

I stroll down the aisles sipping my coffee and singing the lyrics to the songs playing on the loudspeaker. Next, I saunter to the frozen food section where I enjoy the cool breeze whipping through my hair when I open the freezer door to get a box of waffles. And for entertainment, I stop in the greeting card aisle to read the joke birthday cards.

Even though this may sound silly, let me just say that I know people who take mini-vacations very seriously. Like my friend Peggy, the mother of three children, who puts on a black dress every Friday night and spends the evening at a big discount warehouse wandering the aisles and eating free samples as if she were at a cocktail party.

Or my friend Monica, who goes to the gym and reads trashy magazines while peddling the stationary bike just so she can put her children in the free daycare. And then there's my neighbor Julie, who walks really slowly down her driveway to get the mail.

Of course, one of the nice things about mini vacations is that sometimes you don't even have to leave the house to take them. I mean, once the children are asleep you can toss all of the Barbie shoes and Hot Wheels into the toy box, then turn on a talk show or catch up on your reading as if you're living in your own little apartment.

And for those of us with older children, there's always the school PTA which, you might as well know, is really an entire vacation package in disguise—especially since (if you plan it right) you can sign up for so many committees that you'll have somewhere new to go almost every night.

Needless to say, one of the best things about taking mini vacations is that for the most part, they're spontaneous. On top of that, you don't have to figure out how to pack three hundred diapers into a carry-on bag. But despite this, most of my friends without children can't understand why I enjoy going to the restroom by myself as much as, say, spending a weekend in Cabo. And, frankly I don't blame them. There are just some things people have to experience themselves to appreciate.

But remember, next time you go to a store and see a woman with a far away look in her eyes lingering in the paperback book section, tapping her foot to the beat of Muzak and humming softly to herself, for goodness sakes, don't stop to talk. Just keep walking and let her enjoy herself in peace.

She is, after all, on vacation.

$\mathcal{P}$ink and Blue Make . . . Green?

It has come to my attention that there are two types of pregnant women in this world: those who find out the gender of their child as soon as they can and go around calling their stomach "Tommy" or "Jennifer" for the next nine months; and those who refuse to find out the gender of their child one nanosecond before the actual birth, *no matter what.*

Let me just stop right here a minute and say that I in no way advocate one choice over the other. I firmly believe it's a personal choice that should be left to the parents. But that said, what I don't understand is why the very same people who refuse to look at the sonogram screen in the doctor's office are perfectly fine with relying on Old Wives Tales to predict their baby's gender.

Take, for instance, my friend Linda who tried to find out what she was having by twirling a needle on a string over her stomach.

"It's a girl," she announced gleefully over the phone. "The needle spun in circles."

She was so sure, in fact, that she painted the nursery pink and stenciled ballerina bunnies on the walls. But as luck would have it, when she tried it again two months later the needle moved in a straight line, mostly between the refrigerator and the television set—and everyone knows what *that* means.

But that's not all. Once, when my friend Julie was pregnant with her second child, she heard she could tell what she was having if there was a white line above her top lip.

"Can you come over," she said frantically over the phone, "I think I have a lip line. But I can't tell if it's really a 'line-line' or a pale wrinkle or a milk mustache left over from the bowl of cereal I ate for breakfast."

The big drawback to this method is that once we determined that it was indeed a bona fide line-line, we had absolutely no idea if it meant she was having a girl or a boy.

And, oh all right, then there was the time I tried the Chinese Lunar calendar method. But just for the record, I want you to know that it's a highly respected system based on a complicated numerical combination of the father's birth year, lucky elements, planetary rotation, and the number of his favorite local take-out. (But I could be wrong about this.)

What I didn't see coming was that to get an accurate result, you need to be fairly good at math. So after spending hours adding and subtracting cycle scores and percentages and all that, I came out with a bizarre triple negative number that's only been seen on university entrance exams and certain Wall Street corporate earnings reports.

But that's just the kind of answer I usually get whenever I try to walk on the mystical side of life.

The other day my friend Linda (who's now six months pregnant) said to me over coffee, "I've tried everything. According to the needle test I'm having a boy, the lunar calendar says I'm having a girl, the heartbeat test falls somewhere between a boy and a girl, and the Drano test doesn't say anything at all, but it smells really, really bad." She sighed. "I don't know what to believe anymore."

"Then why don't you save yourself the trouble and just ask your doctor?" I asked.

"What?" she said. "And spoil the mystery? Every parent knows that the gender of your child is the one greatest mystery in the world. Why would I want to go and ruin it?"

Granted, I could've mentioned that she was a person who just mixed urine with Drano to see if it would make green, but instead I said simply, "You're right."

With pregnant women, sometimes that's the best way.

Noticing Notices

Make no mistake about it. Sending your child out into the world creates all sorts of surprising parental responsibilities. And I don't mean things like making sure they're wearing shoes or teaching them to look both ways before crossing the street or anything like that. Oh, no. That's a given. I mean things that you've never even thought about before. Like, for instance, keeping up with all of the paperwork. Because you see, as the parent of school-aged children, you're in charge of all the notices they'll bring home. And not just one or two mind you. Piles and piles of them filled with all sorts of important times and dates that you're supposed to keep and refer back to when needed. But take it from me, you won't.

One of the main problems with notices is that they tend to disappear just when you need them most. And don't waste your time looking—you'll never find them. This is because they have, in fact, disappeared into thin air, not to be seen again until the day *after* whatever-it-was-you-needed-to-be-reminded-about had happened.

You'd think this problem would be resolved by finding a practical place to keep notices. You would think. But the other tricky thing about notices is that they don't stay in one place. Oh, they'll start out innocently enough, lying on the kitchen table or on the desk next to the phone, but they'll somehow end up in mysterious, unthinkable places—like behind the sofa cushions or in the backyard underneath the cat's water dish. No one knows for certain why this happens. My children claim that the wind blows them there, while others say it's the result of running a shoddy, haphazard kind of household. But my theory is that almost the instant you receive them, notices become a special kind of Glorified Scratch Paper.

Which is exactly what happened to the very, *very* important notice about the mandatory rehearsals for my daughter's annual violin recital.

"It didn't stand a chance, you see," I explained to her music teacher. "The very nanosecond the notice came out of the backpack, it was put on the Specially Designated Spot on the Refrigerator Door. And then it was used for several rounds of tic-tac-toe and as a canvas for a crayon sketch of our house being swallowed by a big, purple sun. After that it disappeared completely, only to mysteriously reappear days later underneath the sofa. But by then a wad of gum was sticking to it and all I could make out was the word "vznxl," and something with a "2.""

I could tell by the look on his face that he wasn't the sort of person who had this kind of trouble at his house.

Of course, there are parents out there who *can* keep track of their notices and flyers. They're the people who are always on time for kick-offs, never miss a PTA meeting, and generally just go around making the rest of us look bad.

Now you might think that with a little bit of effort and organization I, too, could shake off my bad reputation and mend my ways. Fat chance.

Once I tried putting every single notice my children brought home into a Special Red Folder. But despite my best efforts, the paperwork refused to remain in its designated spot. Day after day I'd catch the soccer schedule roaming through the house aimlessly until I eventually cornered it upstairs in my daughter's bedroom disguised as a camping tarp underneath Malibu Barbie's tent. Just try explaining that.

Then there was the time I resorted to luring notices out of hiding by going through each room in the house crying loudly, "IT'S TOO BAD THE CUB SCOUT PICNIC HAPPENED *YESTERDAY, AND WE MISSED IT!*"

Now I bet you're thinking that this doesn't sound like anything a sane and rational person would do. And you're right. But we all know there's nothing sane or rational about keeping track of notices; or, for that matter, about being a parent. Now if I could just get that in writing.

Garage Junk

Occasionally the difference between men and women astounds me.

Take, for example, the garage. Call me naïve, but I've always thought of a garage as a nice convenient place to store big objects like, say, a car. My husband, on the other hand, has always considered it to be more of an extra closet, the perfect place to keep everything he owns that doesn't qualify to live inside the house. Stuff like peace-sign cement cinder blocks, wrenches, cans of motor oil, rusty nails, burned out circuit boards and eight-track tape players. In other words: junk.

Okay, I'll admit it. We all have some junk in our lives. Even sane, logical people have things they'll never get rid of. My friend Barb's husband (an educated man with a Master's degree in business) is emotionally attached to cases of sticky notes he kept from his first job twelve years ago. My friend Linda has boxes and boxes of used gift bows stored in her garage.

But face it, you can't go around saving everything.

So I dropped the bomb one morning over breakfast. I turned and looked my husband straight in the eye and said, "Today I'm going to clean out the garage."

He smiled at me, clearly missing the magnitude of my decision. "Why?"

"So we can get into the car each morning without running through the sprinklers," I said.

"But . . ."

"Don't get all worked up," I said. "I'm only going to get rid of all the stuff we don't need anymore. I saw how to do it on a talk show."

"A talk show?"

I hadn't wanted him to know about this part actually, but I'd seen this idea on a talk show. I'd started watching it thinking that cleaning, along with transvestite cross-dressers and people who marry barnyard animals, is a topic I could make fun of. But halfway through the show when they started discussing how de-cluttering your surroundings can change your life, I realized they were speaking directly to me.

"I'm just going to relocate some stuff to, well, Goodwill," I continued.

"What stuff? *My* stuff?"

I could see he wasn't ready for the full impact so I proceeded slowly.

"Oh, just a few things we don't need anymore. Like maybe the five VCR's that haven't worked since sometime in 1987 and the disco ball with the black light."

I could tell by the way he was staring at me that this wasn't going to be easy. Clearly, if I wanted to make any sort of progress, I'd have to have a better plan.

So I called my friend Julie, the only person I knew who could fit two entire cars into her garage.

"How do you do it?" I asked her. "How do you keep your garage so clean?"

"Baby steps," she said simply. "Start with the less obvious junk and gradually work it around the garage towards the trunk of your car. After about three days, toss it in. By the time you get rid of it, he won't even notice it's gone."

Now a good person would think, "Wait a minute! This is sneaky and just plain wrong. I can't go around manipulating people's property this way.

A medium-good person would think, "Well, I feel bad but, hey, something has to be done."

Me, I waited until my husband went to work, then moved his spare manual lawn mower over by the water softener. Then I scooted his box of fishing lures towards the water heater and started dispersing old computer parts on the shelves above the door.

However, once I got started I discovered two particular drawbacks to this system. The first was that at this rate, the garage would be cleared sometime in 2076 and I'd be too old to enjoy it. The second was that deep down, sneaking around this way just feels, well, wrong.

That said, I want you to know I did discover one enormous perk: by rearranging his junk I accidentally created more space in the garage. Not enough to park a car mind you, but enough to hold, say, a nice big box of maternity clothes, all of my college textbooks, and a pair of worn out Birkenstocks.

Not that I plan on keeping them or anything.

Renegade Mom

This is going to be a sad story about a mother of two who has hit rock bottom. Now if you're the type of person who's always on time for the carpool, remembers to attend PTA meetings, and balances your checkbook, just move along quietly down the page. This story is not for you. If, on the other hand, you're the type of mother who arrives in the school parking lot as the morning bell rings, forgets birthdays, and routinely loses permission slips, read on. You'll soon feel a lot better about yourself.

You see, yesterday, in the rush to get my children out the door on time, I sent my five-year-old son to school without his teddy bear. Now, of course, this may not seem like such a bad problem to you. However, yesterday was the annual teddy bear picnic, which means, as you've probably figured out, that every kindergartner gets to bring his or her favorite teddy bear to school.

Oh, I know what you're thinking. You're thinking that only the worst kind of parent could leave her child bear-less. And believe me, you're absolutely right. But before you start writing letters and calling the authorities and all that, I want you to know that the minute I realized my mistake, I threw myself at my son's feet and begged for forgiveness.

"Mom, it's okay," he shrugged. "Stop crying. There were extras."

But let's face it. Even though everyone was nice about it, I still feel guilty. Besides, we all know what's really going on here. Any request for a child to bring something to school is really the teacher's way of seeing exactly what kind of parent you are. And now I'm branded for the rest of the year as the kind of irresponsible mother who does nothing but lay around the house in pajamas watching daytime talk shows and drinking beer out of a brown paper bag.

Oh, I could've made excuses. Like we had an out-of-state emergency and didn't have time to get the bear, or that it had fallen out of the car window on the way to school.

But that wouldn't be true. Besides, it could happen to anybody, right? RIGHT?

In my defense, I'm really a good parent. It's just that sometimes I end up making the wrong impression.

Like the time I took my kids to the library. Everything was going great until we got to the checkout desk and I couldn't find my card. This meant that my information had to be looked up in the computer. So they punched in our phone number and brought up my entire borrowing history and let me tell you, I bet criminals in the federal penitentiary have a cleaner record than I do.

First of all, it listed all of the times I'd requested a new card. Then it said I'd lost a magazine. On top of that, it showed I owed a fine for a book I'd checked out sometime in 1993.

Naturally I didn't remember any of this, but something told me that the librarian wasn't going to trust a person like me with any more books until I paid up. So I wrote a check. But then they needed to see my ID, which, as luck would have it, was somewhere at home—possibly marking my place in the missing book. In less than five minutes, I went from being a suburban mother of two with an A+ credit rating and a good dental plan to being an irresponsible menace to society. I mean, if this type of thing can happen in America, no one is safe.

Then, of course, there was the time I forgot to send a giant rock to school so my seven-year-old daughter could make a Christmas paperweight. Not to mention an empty baby food jar for a snow scene and a flurry of late permission slips.

And once I even returned a library movie to the video rental store and a rented video to the library. Now, try explaining *that*.

But the important thing here is that no matter how bad I look to everyone else, my family forgives me.

I know one day my life will slow down and I'll turn my reputation around. But until then, I'm stocking my trunk with spare rocks, empty baby food jars, extra pencils, crayons, glue sticks, library cards, copies of permission slips, and, oh yeah, a stuffed bear or two.

Just in case.

$\mathcal{M}$y Eight-Year-Old Teenager

Like most parents, I fantasize about having a loving, nurturing relationship with my child.

So during the first seven years of my daughter's life, I tried to follow all of the recommendations from the top childhood experts. I spent quality time with her at interesting places, used positive reinforcement and praise to build high self-esteem, and created a strong family bond by fostering a sense of love and togetherness. I also taught her how to play a mean game of jacks.

I imagined us, when she got older, being like a family on the cover of a magazine or in a television sitcom.

Then she turned eight.

Now, there's nothing really wrong with being eight. I've always thought if it as a nice, non-threatening age, except I can't get used to the fact that one moment my daughter is hosting a tea party with her dolls; and the next, covering most of her body parts with temporary tattoos.

I was caught completely off guard until a close friend explained to me that "eight" isn't really an age at all; it's more of a holding pattern between childhood and adolescence.

At first I tried to ignore the early signs—like her refusal to hold my hand when we crossed the street or her request that I stop standing up in the bleachers and yelling things like, "BUBBLE GUM AND TOOTIE FRUITY, WE GOT THE POWER TO WHUP YOUR BOOTIE! YEE HAW!" during her soccer games.

I finally got the message when she began interrogating me as we got ready to go to her new classroom for third grade orientation.

"Mom, I don't want to hurt your feelings," she said, "but you aren't going to wear your long denim skirt again are you?"

"Yes, in fact, I am. Why?"

"Oh, no reason," she said. "But you're not going to wear the matching floppy hat with the big silk flowers, too. Right?"

"Well, I was considering . . ."

"Or the Birkenstocks?"

"But . . ."

"And please don't go and ask all those questions about things like grades and stuff, okay?"

"Well, I . . ."

"You know," she said, matter-of-factly, "my desk is real small and it would be hard for you to sit in it wearing a long skirt and all. But there are a lot of bigger chairs in the back of the room." She smiled brightly.

The more she talked, the more I grew suspicious that a teenager had somehow invaded the eight-year-old body of my little girl.

After all, how could this be coming from the same person who since she was three thought I was the prettiest, coolest, and smartest person in the world?

This couldn't possibly be the same girl who once insisted on wearing her fairy princess costume, accessorized with a pair of furry pink plastic high heels and a purple feather boa, everywhere she went for six months.

Or the very child who just the other day had looked up at me with both arms outstretched and shouted, "Turn me around and spin me, Mom!"

I finally arrived at her classroom: a broken, silent, hatless woman wearing a pair of plain jeans and modern shoes. I obediently sat in one of the "big chairs" in the back of the room along with the other hatless parents, and tried to look as if I didn't actually know anyone in the third grade—I had just wandered in off the street to take a little rest.

As the school year progressed, I wasn't sure how I felt about the two versions of my daughter, especially since I could never be quite sure which one I was dealing with.

Like the time I sat down in the recliner and was stabbed by a bottle of contraband Fire Engine Red nail polish. I waited until my daughter wasn't looking, then carefully slipped it into the trash. Two days later I found it in the bathroom behind the soap dispenser, so I hid it in my medicine cabinet. She found it and put it on her dresser. I stuffed it into the big garbage can in the garage and gloated over my parental victory—until she fished it out and painted it on her toenails.

Shortly after that, she came home from school, put one hand on her hip and announced that if anyone should need her; she would be upstairs in her "apartment" doing her homework.

At first I didn't know what to make of it. Then I decided to go along with it since referring to her bedroom as her apartment would make the rest of the house mine, at least in theory, without having to wait ten more years.

I fantasized about sitting all alone in my spotless living room, wearing my long denim skirt and floppy hat, belting out songs like, "Tie a Yellow Ribbon around the Old Oak Tree," with all the windows open. And standing up to shout soccer cheers anytime I felt like it. Or being able to watch all of the talk shows and listen to seventies music on the stereo. Maybe even dance!

But as she closed the door behind her, I wasn't sure if I was ready for all that freedom yet. Especially since deep down, I can hardly believe the baby I used to crochet sweaters for wants to wear designer jeans and trendy shoes. I feel sad thinking that upstairs, in her eighty-five square foot, pastel pink apartment, my daughter is lost somewhere between fairy tales and training bras.

But occasionally my little girl returns.

Like the other day when (after three hours of not speaking to me because I wouldn't let her wear lipstick to school) she looked at me with big, innocent eyes and asked me to tell her again what color gown the Tooth Fairy wore—and what exactly she did with all those extra teeth. And if I was *"absolutely sure"* that she would be able to find our house, much less the tooth hidden underneath her pillow.

I smiled and reassured her, like so many times before, that the Tooth Fairy couldn't possibly miss our house since it was the only one on the block with Christmas lights on it in July. I told her, once again, that the Tooth Fairy wears a translucent blue gown with silver glitter sparkles and a magic golden crown. And definitely no lipstick. And I explained that she flits about collecting teeth strictly as a hobby. Her real job is being the chief executive of a lucrative denture company, which she earned by doing her math homework without her mother pestering her, and by going to a good four-year college. But I can tell she doesn't really believe me.

In fact, I almost expect her to blurt out, "No *way*," lunge for my lipstick, and announce that she has at last found a bigger apartment in a trendier neighborhood and will be moving out on her own first thing tomorrow morning.

But instead, she stretches her arms up to me, and shouts, "Turn me around and spin me, Mom!"

I smile, then put my arms around her and hold her tight as we spin.

All You Remember

All you remember about your child being an infant is the incredible awe you felt at the precious miracle you'd created. You remember having plenty of time to bestow all your wisdom and knowledge. You thought your child would take all of your advice and make fewer mistakes and be much smarter than you were.

Then you wished for your child to hurry and grow up.

All you remember about your child being two is never using the restroom alone or getting to watch a movie that wasn't full of talking animals. You recall afternoons talking on the phone while crouched behind the shoetree in the bedroom closet, and being convinced your child would be the first Ivy League college student to graduate wearing training pants. You remember being at the ceremony and worrying about the bag of M&M's melting in your pocket and ruining your good dress.

You wished for your child to be more independent.

All you remember about your child being five is the first day of school and finally having the house all to yourself. You remember joining the PTA, and being elected president when you left the meeting for a few minutes to use the restroom. You remember being asked, "Is Santa real?" and saying "Yes," because he had to be for a little bit longer. You remember shaking the sofa cushions for loose change so the Tooth Fairy could come and take away your child's first lost tooth.

You wished for your child to have all permanent teeth.

All you remember about your child being seven is the carpool schedule. You learned to apply makeup in two minutes and brush your teeth in the rearview mirror because the only time you had to yourself was when you were stopped at red lights. You considered painting your car yellow and posting a "taxi" sign on the lawn next to the garage door. You remember people staring at you the few times you were out of the car, because you kept flexing your foot and making acceleration noises.

You wished for the day your child would learn how to drive.

All you remember about your child being ten is managing the school fund-raisers. You sold wrapping paper for paint, T-shirts for new furniture, and magazine subscriptions for shade trees in the school playground. You remember storing a hundred cases of chocolate candy bars in the garage to sell so the school band could get new uniforms, and how they melted together on an unseasonably warm spring afternoon.

You wished your child would give up playing an instrument.

All you remember about your child being twelve is sitting in the stands during baseball practice and hoping your child's team would strike out fast because you had more important things to do at home. The coach didn't understand how busy you were.

You wished baseball season would be over soon

All you remember about your child being fourteen is being asked not to stop the car in front of the school in the morning. You had to drive two blocks further and unlock the doors without coming to a complete stop. You remember not getting to kiss your child good-bye or talking to them in front of their friends.

You wished your child would be more mature.

All you remember about your child being sixteen is loud music and undecipherable lyrics screamed to a rhythmic beat.

You wished for your child to grow up and leave home—with the stereo.

All you remember about your child being eighteen is thinking about the day she was born, when you had all the time in the world. And as you walk through your quiet house, you wonder where the years went.

And you wish your child hadn't grown up so fast.